SPEED

GUY MARTIN

HOW TO MAKE THINGS GO REALLY FAST

10 9 8 7 6 5 4 3

Published in 2014 by Virgin Books, an imprint of Ebury Publishing. A Random House Group Company

The Random House Group Limited Reg. No. 954009

Addresses for companies within the Random House Group can be found at www.randomhouse.co.uk

A CIP catalogue record for this book is available from the British Library

Penguin Random House is committed to a sustainable future for our business, our readers and our planet. This book is made from Forest Stewardship Council® certified paper.

Designed by Two Associates

Printed and bound in Italy by L. E. G. O. SpA

ISBN 9780753541067

To buy books by your favourite authors and register for offers visit www.randomhouse.co.uk

Photography © Barry Hayden 2014, except for p17 (top) private collection, (bottom) Getty Images/SSPL; p18 (top) Getty Images/Hulton Archive, (bottom) private collection; p20 (top) private collection, (bottom) Corbis/© Bettmann; p21 (top) Corbis, (bottom) Getty Images/Popperfoto; p22 (top) Dutch National Archives, (bottom) Getty Images; p32 Getty Images/iStock; p33 Getty Images/iStock; p54 North One Televsion; p58 North One Televsion; p59 Dave Le Grys; p81 (top and bottom) Getty Images/SSPL; p82 (top) Getty Images/SSPL, (bottom) Getty Images/UIG; p83 (top) Getty Images/Hulton Archive, (middle) Getty Images/Gamma-Keystone, (bottom) private collection; p85 (top) Getty Images/Popperfoto, (bottom) Alan Lassiere; p86 (top) Alan Lassiere, (bottom) Getty Images/SSPL; p87 (top) Getty Images/SSPL, (middle) Getty Images/Gamma-Keystone, (bottom) Royal Aeronautical Society; p89 North One Television; p90 North One Television; p91 North One Television; p92–93 North One Television; p101 North One Television; p102 Getty Images/iStock; p103 Getty Images/iStock; p114 Alan Lassiere; p115 Alan Lassiere; p116–117 Getty Images/iStock; p118–119 Getty Images/iStock; p136 Charlie Magee; p138 Charlie Magee; p139 Getty Images/iStock; p140 Charlie Magee; p141 Charlie Magee; p143 (top) Alamy, (middle) Getty Images/Popperfoto, (bottom) Getty Images; p144 (top) Getty Images/Hulton Archive, (bottom) Getty Images/Hulton Archive; p145 Charlie Magee; p146 Charlie Magee; p148–149 Charlie Magee; p150 Charlie Magee; p151 Charlie Magee; p162–163 Charlie Magee; p164 Getty Images/Encyclopedia Britannica/UIG; p165 Getty Images/DEA Picture Library; p168 North One Television; p169 (top and bottom) North One Television; p170 North One Television; p173 North One Television; p174 North One Television; p184 Charlie Magee; p185 Charlie Magee; p186 (top and bottom) Charlie Magee; p187 Charlie Magee; p188 Charlie Magee; p189 (top and bottom) Charlie Magee; p190–191 Charlie Magee; p192 (top, middle, bottom) Charlie Magee; p193 Charlie Magee; p194–195 Charlie Magee; p196 Charlie Magee; p197 Charlie Magee; p198 Charlie Magee; p199 Charlie Magee; p200–201 Charlie Magee; p207 North One Television; p209 (top) Private Collection, (bottom) copyright Elzbieta Sekowska, 2013/used under license from Shutterstock; p210 (top) copyright Elzbieta Sekowska, 2013/used under license from Shutterstock, (bottom) Alamy/© Liszt Collection; p211 (top) Getty Images/Hulton Archive, (bottom) Corbis/© STR/Keystone; p218 (top and bottom) Crestaphotos.com; p219 North One Television; p220 Crestaphotos.com; p221 (top and bottom) North One Television; p222 North One Television; p224 North One Television; p226 North One Television; p227 (all) North One Television; p228–229 North One Television; p253 Charlie Magee.

Diagrams and illustrations by Dominic Cooper at Two Associates.

Every reasonable effort has been made to contact copyright holders of material reproduced in this book. If any have inadvertently been overlooked the publishers would be glad to hear from them and make good in future editions any errors or omissions brought to their attention.

Contents

Introduction

'Speed. Danger. The two things go together like bread and butter, or trucks and trailers, or bits 'n' bobs ... or do they?'

PEOPLE often assume that I race motorbikes because I'm addicted to speed, but that's not strictly true. Speed on its own isn't always so exciting. On a racing motorbike I can do over 180 mph, which is fast, but not as fast as the airliners that we all climb aboard to fly off on holiday. Modern passenger jets can cruise at between 500 and 600 mph, but sitting in an aeroplane like that for hours on end isn't very exciting, is it? In fact, passengers read books, watch movies or have a kip to pass the time – travelling at over 500 mph can be really boring! It's certainly not dangerous. You might be thundering through the sky six miles high, but you can find all sorts of statistics to show that flying is the safest form of long-distance travel. The fact is, sitting strapped into an airline seat watching an in-flight movie, you don't even have much of a clue that you are going fast. You can't actually feel the speed in an airliner, but you certainly can on a motorbike. It's when you can feel the speed that you get a sense of danger – and when the two come together there is nothing else in the world that compares.

When I came off my bike during the Isle of Man TT in 2010, the feeling when I knew that everything was going wrong and that I wasn't going to be able to hold on to the bike – at 170 mph – was unbeatable. That was a proper buzz. Those few moments between being in control of what I was doing, then losing control, and the instant between crashing and almost dying were intense. That's the ultimate feeling of danger. Money can't buy that feeling – it's priceless. I like the idea that I have to get things right when I'm racing. Fail to get it right and that's it, game over, I'm dead. Racing motorbikes may be the ultimate thrill for me, but it's not the only way to have fun with a bit of speed and a bit of danger. Racing mountain

bikes is another passion of mine. Charging down a hillside at 50 or 60 mph, you rely on your skill and judgement to keep you out of trouble. You feel every bump, twist and jolt that the mountain throws at you, and you have to be able to cope with it or you will very quickly become part of the scenery, with a few broken bones thrown into the bargain.

Being able to feel the speed was what inspired the challenges that I attempted for the TV shows that we made, and which we look at in greater detail in this book. I'm a great believer in setting myself goals, and I like to think that, once I've a goal to aim for, I'll do whatever it takes to achieve it. Problems are part of the challenge and you have to work your way through them. If you were to be put off by every little problem life throws at you, you'd get nowt done.

Just get on with it, is what I say – but, even though I might sometimes seem like a spanner short of a full set, I'm not daft enough to think that I can do everything all on my own. It takes the backing of an entire team for me to go racing motorbikes, and when I set myself the challenges that you can read about here, I needed some really talented people backing me up.

The idea was, as you are about to find out, to look at different forms of speed and the science that I would have to learn about to prepare for the speed challenges, as well as the skills that I would have to master to come out on top. In all of the challenges, I would get a proper feeling of speed and, in some more than others, I can tell you that I was definitely getting a bit of that danger buzz!

Riding Britain's Fastest Bike meant learning about slipstreaming to minimise drag, and that was to become something of a common theme throughout the challenges. Achieving high speeds always means defeating drag, whether you are in the air, in the water or on dry land. It was fascinating to learn about how Mother Nature had, in so many different ways, tackled the problems we were facing and, as always, I was really grateful to all of those who put up with my questions, showing huge patience in explaining to me how a wing works, why air is really just like water, or how lizards manage to run across ponds!

I discovered a few things about myself during the challenges, too. On the Britain's Fastest Bike and the Human Powered Aircraft jobs, I was looking forward to doing some hardcore cycling, and found out that my pedalling power wasn't quite as awesome as I had thought! Despite the fact that I put in plenty of miles most days on my way to and from work, I had a lot to do to bring myself up to scratch. On the Hydroplaning Motorbike challenge I discovered that doing acrobatics off the front of my bike into a lake can make falling into water feel like slamming into concrete. Racing downhill on a sled made me realise that I hadn't lost that feeling of pure excitement you get when you're a kid, sliding down a snowy hillside on a bin-bag. To find it, all I had to do was go a little bit faster!

I hope that everyone who put so much time and effort into working with me on the TV series enjoyed the whole experience as much as I did, and I hope that, when you read this book, you will be able to share in the fun and maybe learn a few things that you never knew before.

Speed and danger don't always go together, but it's proper fun when they do.

Britain's Fastest Bike

The Challenge

'100 mph on a pushbike? Surely not!'

LIKE most people, I started riding a bike when I was still a kid. I had a Raleigh Chopper and a Raleigh Mustang before I started moving on to really serious stuff like the Whyte 46 mountain bike or the Cotic that I use every day. That's what I call a proper bike. It goes pretty much everywhere with me and I ride it to work. I can easily get up to 30 mph on a normal road – a lot faster on a downhill stretch – and keeping up with traffic is never a problem. So when they told me that I was going to get the chance to ride a fast pushbike, I thought, 'All right – but I do that every day.'

Then they told me that I was going to ride a pushbike at over 100 mph, and my ears pricked up. Was that really possible? On a racing motorbike at the Isle of Man TT we can average 130 mph round the course, which means hitting over 180 mph at times, but that's with a race-tuned engine screaming away beneath you. With only pedal power to rely on, can you get to 100 mph, or more? This is on the flat, remember, not downhill with gravity lending you a helping hand. 100 mph on a pushbike? Surely not!

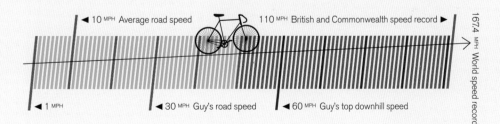

◄ 10 MPH Average road speed   110 MPH British and Commonwealth speed record ►

167.4 MPH World speed record

◄ 1 MPH   ◄ 30 MPH Guy's road speed   ◄ 60 MPH Guy's top downhill speed

As incredible as it sounds, the British and Commonwealth bicycle speed record was set in 1986 at 110 mph. The record had remained unbeaten for 27 years. I wasn't only to be pedalling as fast as I could – I had a target to aim for. Once I realised that others had ridden at over 100 mph, nobody was going to stop me having a go as well.

It was, of course, more complicated than just hopping on a bike and pedalling like mad. I had a lot to learn about the effects that high speeds have on bicycles and their riders. For a start, it would not be possible for me just to jump on my Cotic and go for it. I could pedal like the clappers till the cows came home and I still wouldn't hit 100 mph. It is a lot different to riding a motorbike where you generally have as much power as you need on tap. The gearing on the cycle for the speed attempt would be so high that the pedals would be impossible for me to turn if I tried to start off under my own muscle power. Neither could I, or any other rider, cope with pedalling against the air resistance I would experience when I was doing over 'the ton'. I was going to have to learn about slipstreaming and motor pacing. How brilliant do you think all that sounded? I could hardly wait.

Reaching more than 100 mph on a pushbike was going to take a lot of hard work, but I've never been shy of that. It wasn't going to be easy but that's all part of the fun. After all, if it was easy everybody would be doing it, wouldn't they?

Below: A glimpse of the very special bicycle we built for the challenge.

Right: I didn't want the down draught from the TV crew's chopper anywhere near me when I was pedalling at 100 mph!

Discovering the World of Motor Pacing

Ever since bicycles first started to appear in the nineteenth century people have wanted to make them go faster.

WHEN I visited the Scottish Cycle Museum at Drumlanrig Castle with my mate Mave, we borrowed a penny farthing and a copy of an 1839 MacMillan cycle and our first thought was 'Let's see how fast they can go!' So we had a race. The penny farthing, which came along around 30 years after the MacMillan, was far quicker and it was with bicycles like these that the first official races were run in 1868. English rider James Moore is credited with winning the first race at Parc Saint-Cloud in Paris, riding a bike with iron tyres!

Racing against other cyclists is all very well, but it's not the same as seeing how fast you can go – or how fast you dare to go. Sitting on top of the big wheel of a penny farthing didn't feel like the best racing position I had ever been in on two wheels when I tried it, but for F. L. Dodds in 1876 there was no choice. He set the first record for the distance covered in one hour – almost 16 miles. Clever Mr Dodds used a team of other riders to pace him, riding around the grounds of Cambridge University. Riding behind another cyclist, Dodds was able to maintain a high speed without using as much energy as the guy in front of him because he was riding in the slipstream. Slipstreaming was something that I knew a bit about from motorcycle racing. I knew how bikers use it, but I was going to have to delve into the science of how and why it worked, and we'll be looking at that a little later. The riders creating the slipstream for Dodds dropped out after a few minutes, to be replaced by someone with fresh legs in much the same way that you may have seen cycle racers doing during the Olympic Games. The team tucks in behind the leader, who takes the strain for a while before veering off up the banking in the velodrome and swooping down to rejoin the team at the back, leaving someone else to take over the tough job at the front.

> It was thrilling stuff to watch, mainly, as in all sports where there's an element of danger involved, because if it all went pear-shaped and somebody came a cropper he might not live to tell the tale.

Of course, using that pacing technique, you can only go as fast as the fastest rider. That was fine for Mr Dodds in 1876 when he was trying to set a record for distance covered in an hour, but for a flat-out top speed you needed a pace rider who can go much faster than you can, which is a problem if the pace man has only the same muscle power as you do. The answer was to use more legs to give more muscle power on the pace bike. Two riders on a tandem were used, then three on a triplet, with up to five on a quintuplet bicycle hammering around a track ahead of the would-be record breaker. Bicycle and tyre manufacturers sponsored race teams and record breakers, just as car manufacturers would later do, to show the public how fast and reliable their machines were.

John William Stocks was one of the early bicycle stars, riding an Ariel cycle with a team of Dunlop professional cyclists on a series of quintuplets pacing him to achieve 32 miles and 448 yards in one hour in 1897 on a track at Crystal Palace in London. Stocks was stopped for speeding on the Great North Road in 1899 in an Ariel motorised tricycle, ironically probably going slower than he did around the cycle track as the 1¾ horsepower Ariel would have been starting to run out of legs before it reached 30 mph!

The motorbike, however, was to change the way that high-speed pacing worked. As more powerful engines were developed, motorbikes became faster and motor pacing developed into a huge spectator sport in both Europe and America. By 1903 cyclists like Bobby Walthour were racing behind motorbikes at speeds of over 60 mph. The motorbikes were specially designed so that the rider sat right back over the rear wheel, with the handlebars on long extensions to allow him to steer the thing. Sitting that far back, and sitting bolt upright, he provided the windbreak for the cyclist pounding away at the pedals just inches behind him. Some pacing machines had two riders, one crouched low over the handlebars to steer the bike and the other perched high over the rear wheel, controlling the engine.

It wasn't record motor pacing record attempts that the crowds flocked to see, but actual races with motorbike-and-cyclist teams pitted against each other on the same track at the same time. It was thrilling stuff to watch, mainly, as in all sports where there's an element of danger involved, because if it all went pear-shaped and somebody came a cropper he might not live to tell the tale. Bobby Walthour was American Motor Pacing Champion in 1903 when he was invited to

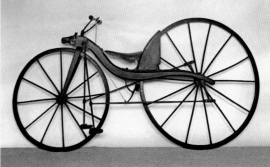

Top: James Moore (right), winner of the 1869 Paris-Rouen race, pictured with the runner-up Jean-Eugene-Andre Castera.

Bottom: The 1839 MacMillan bicycle was driven by levers rather than a chain.

LES SPORTS. — STAYERS ET ENTRAINEURS
MICHAËL, *Stayer Américain, entraîné par* DANGLARD

Top: Welsh miner Arthur Linton became an international star in the early 1890s.

Bottom: Another Welshman, Jimmy Michael, seen here riding behind a motor pacing bike, was Arthur Linton's greatest rival.

race in Paris against the top French cyclists before going on to Berlin to face the German champions. That one tour earned him $15,000 in prize money, which is about $373,000 or £232,000 in today's money. He was earning more in a season than the highest-paid baseball stars of the day but he was taking huge risks to make his money. I know from the tumbles that I've had how easy it is to lose control at speed. You can be on top of your game and judging everything to perfection, but accidents do still happen. The motorbikes used for motor pacing in Walthour's day had a frame sticking out behind supporting a roller bar to stop the cyclist's front wheel from hitting the motorbike's back wheel, but that and a basic helmet were all the safety gear that they had. Walthour came off his bike many times, breaking his collar bone – one of the most common injuries for cycle racers – 28 times on the right and 18 times on the left. Add to that about 30 broken ribs and more stitches in his face than Frankenstein's monster and you can see how much these guys craved the speed and the danger. Some of them paid for it with their lives.

At the opening of the Charles River race track in Boston on 30 May 1903, Bobby raced against his toughest rival, Harry Elkes, who had been American champion before Bobby took the title from him. There were two other riders in the 20-mile race, where the cyclists thundered round the track in front of 15,000 spectators. Elkes pushed the pace faster and faster until his chain snapped, smashing into the spokes of his back wheel and destroying it. Elkes was flung from the bike and died instantly when he was run over by one of the other motorbike pacers. If the noise of the motorbikes, the smell of the exhausts, the thrill of the speed and the sight of the cyclists riding within touching distance was what the crowds were after, they could have that at any of the races whether they were sprints or endurance race. If what they wanted was to see death and destruction, on the other hand – and there's no doubt that this is part of what draws people to watch high-speed motorsport – then the newly opened race track in Berlin's Botanical Gardens in July 1909 was the place to be. A pacing machine blew a tyre, skidding across the track. Another machine swerved to avoid it and then took off, out of control, hurtling over the barrier into the crowd, where it exploded, killing nine spectators and injuring 52.

Despite the dangers, or maybe, in a way, because of them, motor pacing continued to grow in popularity in all its various forms. Races were run as sprints, or over set distances, or as endurance events over 24 hours or even several days. Motor pacing wasn't confined to race tracks, either. Endurance races were run on public roads, with the most famous, the Bordeaux to Paris race, first run in 1891. The race was supposed to last for days and the organisers had arranged food and lodgings for the competitors, but English racer George Pilkington Mills saw nothing in the rules that made him think he had to stop for a kip, so he raced on through the night, as did the rest of the British team. They made do with short stops for food and kept going, with George Pilkington Mills arriving first in Paris, 26 hours 36 minutes and 25 seconds after leaving Bordeaux. Other riders were still coming in two days later.

Along with the motor paced races came the thing that interested me most – motor paced speed records. That, after all, was what I was going to be tackling. One of the first major records was set by Charles Minthorn Murphy in 1899. Murphy was a proper, tough New Yorker who claimed to have cycled the

equivalent of almost 100 mph on static rollers and that he could cycle as fast as any man-made machine. The Long Island Railroad Company decided to let Murphy prove his boasts and they laid 10-inch wide (250 mm) boards lengthways between the tracks on a two-mile stretch of their railway between Babylon and Farmingdale on New York's Long Island. With the sleepers covered, this made a perfect, flat surface for Murphy to ride on – or so they thought.

The railway company built a special fairing on to the back of one of their carriages, a kind of open-backed shed with a roof and walls that extended down to the rails. This was to provide a protected slipstream enclosure for Murphy to ride in. Their aim was to crack the 60 mph barrier, covering a measured mile in less than one minute. As I have discovered with all of the challenges that I've attempted, nothing ever goes entirely according to plan, and poor Murphy, riding behind a steam locomotive, was to come across some unexpected problems. On their first run the 29-year-old quickly discovered that the perfectly flat surface he thought he'd be riding on turned into a mini rollercoaster once they were underway. The weight of the locomotive and carriage ahead of him depressed the rails and sleepers, which then rose back into place again, creating an undulating effect. It was enough to make most people feel sea sick, but Murphy didn't have time to think of that; he was too busy dealing with being shot-blasted by hot cinders, sparks and dust thrown up from underneath the train. Steam, smoke and sparks from a locomotive don't only spew out of the smoke stack, there's a fair amount ends up dumped on the track, too, as Murphy found out the hard way! On their first run they covered the mile in one minute and eight seconds, mainly because the train failed to get over 60 mph. Murphy was forced

Top: Bobby Walthour in 1903 – one of the highest-paid athletes of the time.

Bottom: Charles Murphy pedalling away behind the train to earn his nickname 'Mile-a-Minute Murphy'.

to go for it again, and this time was so badly affected by the flying debris that he fell behind, dropping back out of the protective fairing. He had to fight his way back from 15 feet (4.5 metres) behind the train, with the slipstream effect of the carriage fairing actually working against him, to get back into the protective 'pocket'. He put in an amazing effort, going faster than the train to catch up, and when the driver applied the brakes at the end of the run Murphy slammed into the back of the carriage. Just as he did so, the official timers and support staff who had been urging him on from the carriage's rear platform reached down to grab him and haul him aboard. Murphy was totally knackered and suffering from burns to his face and hands, but he had covered the measured mile in 57.8 seconds. From then on he became known as 'Mile-a-Minute Murphy' and his time for motor pacing behind a train has never been beaten.

Other world records were set and broken on a pretty regular basis, with some of the most remarkable including Belgian cyclist Leon Vanderstuyft charging around the Montlhéry Velodrome near Paris behind a motorbike at almost 76 mph (122.77 km/h) in 1928. That might not sound too impressive to us nowadays – after all, you and I could go faster than that in something as basic as my old Astra van, and I've got the speeding points on my licence to prove it – but bear in mind that the absolute top speed of the latest Ford Model A in 1928 was just 65 mph, and you can start to appreciate what an achievement that was.

The cycling speed record continued to creep up, with Frenchman Alexis Blanc-Garin taking it to 79.66 mph (128.2 km/h) in 1933, riding behind a motorbike, and another French rider, Albert Marquet, made it to 86.9 mph (139.9 km/h) behind a Cord car – quite an exotic and powerful American model – with a canvas fairing extension on the back providing a protective pocket. Marquet made his record attempt in California in 1937 and it was also in California that yet another French cyclist, Alfred Letourner, took the record to over 100 mph. That was in 1941, while his home country was languishing under the occupation of the Nazis, Letourner proudly flying the flag for France on an American freeway just outside Bakersfield. He rode behind a customised midget racing car that had a shield-style windbreak built onto the back. Three years previously Letourner had done over 91 mph behind a motorbike that was also equipped with a shield.

Once the 100 mph hurdle had been passed, the next landmark was 200 km/h (124.2 mph). The French seemed determined to keep on breaking the record, and it was Jose Meiffret's turn in 1962. Meiffret had broken Letourner's record in 1951 when he rode behind a Talbot on a flat stretch of road near Toulouse, reaching over 109 mph (175 km/h), and the following year he staged another record attempt at the Montlhery circuit where Vanderstuyft had triumphed in 1928. The circuit had been new in 1928, but by 1952 the surface was far from perfect and Meiffret came a cropper when his front wheel fell apart. He suffered five separate fractures to his skull and was not expected to live. But you can't keep a good man down and in 1962, now 48 years old, Meiffret was pushing his pedals behind a Mercedes 300SL sports car on a German autobahn outside Freiberg. The Mercedes had a flat-backed, tent-like structure providing a windbreak for Meiffret, who made it to over 127 mph (204 km/h).

Bonneville Salt Flats, where world speed records have been set in everything from jet-powered cars to motorised bar stools, was

Top: 'Mile-a-Minute Murphy' (left) could do almost 100 mph on static rollers.

Bottom: Huge crowds turned out for motor pacing events like this one at Herne Hill in London in the 1940s.

the venue for the next round of bicycle speed record attempts. American Allan Abbott hit 139 mph (223 km/h) behind a souped-up 1955 Chevrolet in 1973 while US Olympic cyclist John Howard took the record to 152 mph (244 km/h) in 1985, hurtling along behind a specially built dragster. Howard's record stood for the next 10 years until Dutch professional cycle racer Fred Rompelberg – at 50 years old the oldest professional cyclist in the world – hurtled across the Bonneville flats behind a drag racer at 167.04 mph (268.831 km/h). Rompelberg's remains the motor paced cycling absolute speed record.

> The British and Commonwealth bicycle speed record was set on the M42 motorway in 1986 at 110 mph. That was the one for me.

If I was going to go for a record on a bike, I thought it should be more of a home-grown British affair. Bonneville Salt Flats and fancy drag racers are all very well, but what I wanted was something a bit closer to my own heart – a British record, set in Britain on a British-built bike. It wasn't difficult to work out the record to go for. The British and Commonwealth bicycle speed record was set on the M42 motorway in 1986 at 110 mph. That was the one for me.

Top: Dutch champion cyclist Fred Rompelberg competing in 1969. He was to set the World Cycling Absolute Speed Record 26 years later.

Bottom: Bonneville Salt Flats in Utah, USA, where Fred Rompelberg pedalled behind a drag racer at 167.04 mph (286.831 km/h) just four weeks before his 50th birthday.

Right: The best way to start a record attempt is with a nice cup of tea!

The Drag Race
The Science of Slipstreaming

$$Fd = V^2$$

No, it didn't mean much to me at first, either, but that simple equation is something that has been affecting me all my life. It's been affecting you, too, but when I've been racing motorbikes it's been a major problem to be reckoned with. Why? Try looking at it a different way.

What that means is that you can measure the force of drag as being equivalent to your speed multiplied by itself. The faster you go, therefore, the more drag you will experience. Hold that thought while we have a think about what drag really is.

$$Drag = Speed^2$$

Drag Drag

Pedal power provides the force that pushes me forward but, while it looks like there is nothing to stop me, there is plenty of fresh air in the way. The air resists being pushed out of the way. Air resistance is also called 'drag'.

Drag
(Air Resistance)

Force
(Pedal Power)

The air that we breathe is a gas that's made up of a number of different things – mainly nitrogen, oxygen, argon and carbon dioxide. When you breathe in, you are sucking in all of those, along with a bit of water vapour and, if you're unlucky, a few pollutants as well. Air is a kind of chemical soup that encircles the Earth. We don't normally see it or try to look at it, and the air that we breathe, and walk through, is something that we all take so much for granted that most of the time we forget that it's there. Yet it is a substance that can be measured, weighed and sealed in containers, just like water – and if you now start to think of air a bit like water, things will make a lot more sense.

The water in a pond is obviously a liquid, not a gas, but liquids and gases behave in much the same way. We can 'bully' liquids by shoving them out of our way. If you were to walk into a shallow pond, you could walk through it, pushing the water out of your way. In a deeper pond you might have to swim, using your arms to push the water aside, so that you can take its place and move forward. When you walk out the other side of the pond, things get a lot easier because you no longer have to push the water aside. Yet you are still pushing air – that chemical soup – out of your way. There are a couple of basic scientific principles at work here. The first is good old Sir Isaac Newton's

The air that is pushed out of my way, not just over my head but round the sides and below me as well, is compressed in front of me, creating high-pressure air. It then collapses back in behind me, causing turbulence. Immediately behind me, however, there is a pocket of still, low-pressure air.

(High-pressure Air)

Turbulence

Airflow

Slipstream
(Low-pressure Air)

'First Law of Motion', also called the law of inertia, which states that anything that is settled in one place at rest will stay that way unless a force is applied to it to change that situation. Similarly, any object that is on the move will carry on moving at the same speed and in the same direction until a force is applied that changes the way it is moving.

We can regard the air as being at rest, so we have to apply a force, muscle power from our legs, to power our bodies through the air, pushing it out of the way. That's when Newton's 'Third Law of Motion' (we can skip over his second law for the time being) comes into

play. Like everything else we know, air obeys Newton's 'Third Law', which states that for every action there is an equal and opposite reaction. This means that as you push against the air it pushes back at you. You don't notice it when you're walking, but if you start to run you can feel the air pushing back at you. The natural tendency is for air to obey the 'First Law' and stay at rest. To change that situation, we have to apply force and air then obeys the Third Law by resisting with the same amount of force. The air pushing back at you as you try to move forward is what we call air resistance, or 'drag'. In order to dodge that drag, I would have to use a technique called slipstreaming.

Sitting in the Slipstream

The history of cycle racing and record breaking shows us that cyclists have understood about slipstreaming from the very beginning.

HAVING another rider in front of you means that he is doing all the hard work in pushing the air out of the way and, if you tuck in close enough behind him, you can cycle in a pocket of still air, his slipstream, keeping up with him however fast he goes, but putting in only a fraction of the effort that he has to. Think of walking into that blustery wind again. It's much easier if you can crouch down behind someone else, isn't it?

Cyclists in road races like the Tour de France see a reduction in air resistance of up to 35% if they are close enough behind the man in front of them. If they are riding in a closely bunched group called a *peloton* (French for 'little ball'),

the cyclist in the heart of the pack might be benefiting from as much as a 40% reduction in drag.

They use the slipstreaming technique in motor racing, too, where an even more interesting effect emerged in the American NASCAR series. At the Daytona 500 race in 1960, Junior Johnson was struggling in practice when he and his pit team realised that the other teams were hitting top speeds over 20 mph faster than his car could manage. Then Johnson noticed that, if he tucked in close behind one of the faster cars, he could keep up without even using full throttle. The slipstream was helping him to hammer round the circuit faster than he thought was possible in his car. He then used

Below: Because Rider 1 is working hard to force the air aside, he creates a pocket of lower-pressure air behind him. Cycling in this pocket, Rider 2 can easily keep up using far less energy.

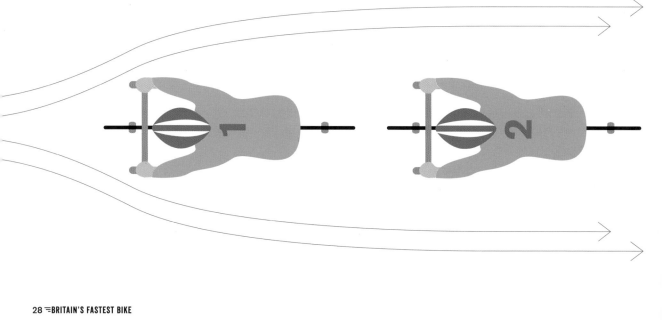

what has become known as a 'slingshot' effect, flooring the accelerator in his car and popping out from the slipstream to overtake. Against the odds, he won the race.

I come across trucks and tractors all the time that I can slipstream behind, helping me to get to work quicker – and home again quicker, too. I keep my wits about me, mind you, to make sure that I don't come a cropper!

Using the 'slingshot' is something that everyone in motorsport now tries to do, but the NASCAR teams also found another use for the slipstream, which they also refer to as the 'draft'. On the circuits at Daytona and Talladega, drivers developed a technique that they called 'bump drafting'. Basically, racing teammates worked together with the rear car driving in the slipstream, then pulling forward to nudge the lead car and shove him along a bit faster. Given that these cars can top 200 mph, deliberately shunting the car in front seems like madness, but two cars 'bump drafting' have been known to run 15 mph faster than they could on their own.

When you see lorries on the motorways rumbling along so close behind one another that you couldn't slip a copy of the Highway Code between them, you can bet that the driver behind is saving fuel by driving in the slipstream of the truck in front. It has been shown that a car driving in the slipstream of a truck can use up to around 40% less fuel. Given that you have to be no more than 10 feet (3 metres) behind the truck, it's certainly not to be recommended. If you're that close, the truck

driver might not be able to see you, and if he slams on his brakes you won't have enough time to react and will plough into the back of him.

For lorry drivers, on the other hand, it's not quite as risky a business. A truck is big enough for the driver in front to see it and, what's more, he quite likes having it there. Why? Because of the way that slipstreaming works, the truck behind deflects some of the turbulent air flow that would normally collapse in behind the leading truck. This air can actually serve to hold the truck back, so with another driver right behind him the lead driver also benefits from a slight fuel saving. They can work together to save each other a few quid!

I have to admit, I've used the slipstream effect as well – on my pushbike. Cycling 35 miles to work every day, I come across trucks and tractors all the time that I can slipstream behind, helping me to get to work quicker – and home again quicker, too. I keep my wits about me, mind you, to make sure that I don't come a cropper!

Above: Me against a racing truck? I wouldn't have a hope – but the truck was key to me beating the record.

1 Tucking in behind Olympic champion Laura Trott, I could feel the benefit of riding in her slipstream.

2 Laura had to put in a lot more effort than me to maintain the same speed. This helped me to preserve my strength as she used up hers.

3 Popping out of the
slipstream 'pocket'
I could immediately feel
the buffeting of the air
Laura was displacing,
and her slipstream was
now working against me.

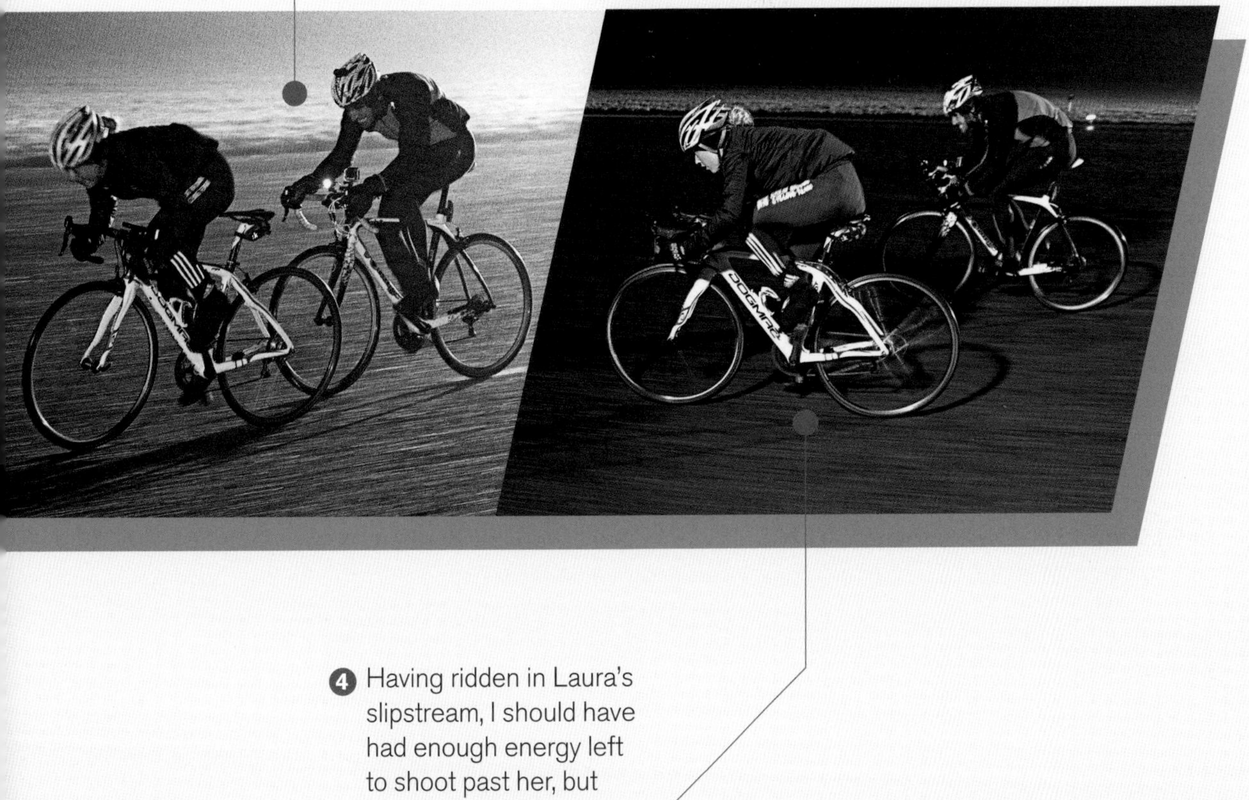

4 Having ridden in Laura's
slipstream, I should have
had enough energy left
to shoot past her, but
I still struggled to catch
her! The girl's good . . .

Natural Slipstreamers

You don't often see a fish riding a bike, so they're not the obvious creatures to turn to when you're looking for tips about making one go faster, but when it comes to streamlining fish have got it sussed.

PRETTY much every sea creature is streamlined. Seals or sea lions, even penguins – clumsy customers on land, but in the water they are fantastically graceful and their streamlining is spot on. Being a slippery shape is all very well, but fish know a thing or two about slipstreaming as well.

A school or shoal of fish may swim together for protection, the idea being that if a bigger fish comes along and decides that it's time for lunch, when it attacks the school can scatter at high speed, making it more difficult for the big fish to pick a target. The school then quickly regroups, but they don't just close up in a random bunch. The fittest, strongest fish swim at the front and the tiddlers follow close behind, staying safe from predators in the middle of the school but also making use of the slipstream effect.

With the larger fish cutting through the water ahead of them, the smaller ones have the benefit of the slipstream and don't have to work so hard to keep up. That way the school can move more quickly without having to slow down to let younger, slower fish stay with the group. The leaders have first sitting for dinner when the school swims into a feeding area, but I suppose that's a perk of the job. You can see perfect examples of animals slipstreaming when you watch horse racing. The Sport of

Kings, they call it – thoroughbred racehorses, like racing cars or motorbikes, costing a king's ransom to buy and maintain. Our own Queen has been mad about horse racing since she was a young lass and as an owner she knows a thing or two about what makes a good runner. One of her favourite races is the Derby, run on Epsom Downs to the south west of London. At the Epsom Derby the horses cover a course that is just over 1½ miles. There are no jumps but they do have to run up a bit of a slope, all at a sprint, so the riders try to grab any advantage they can. At the end of a race, when the horses are galloping for the finish line, they look like they are going flat out but, due to fatigue, they are actually running more slowly than when they first hit top speed. That top speed will probably be about 40 mph, which might not sound very fast to anyone who's ridden a motorbike or driven a car, but imagine trying to control a bike or a car when it is bucking around beneath you and you can't even use your hands to hold on. Instead you have to half-crouch, balanced with your feet in metal loops that are moving around, the only way to keep yourself on board being to grip the beast with your knees!

You need proper skill to ride a racehorse, and a lot of courage. Not many champion jockeys can say that they've never taken a tumble, and most of them have memories of broken bones and the scars to prove it. Staying on board your racehorse, of course, is just the beginning. If you can manage that, then you have to guide your horse into position about eight feet (roughly 2.5 metres) behind the horse in front in order to save energy for that final dash to the finishing post. When the horses are flagging, if you have tucked into the slipstream of the horse and rider in front, your horse may have been able to keep up using less effort than the leader. He might still have some gas in his tank. You then have to judge the right moment to make a break for the line, popping out of the slipstream and urging your horse to use up his extra energy reserves to gallop into the lead.

Slipstreaming during a horse race can reduce drag to such an extent that a horse can put in a time which, when averaged over the whole race, is 2% faster. That might not sound much, but it can mean the difference between winning and coming fourth or fifth.

It's a safe bet, then, that Her Majesty understands all about slipstreaming!

Below: A school of fish swim together for protection. The bigger, stronger fish swim at the front and the smaller, weaker fish follow in the slipstream.

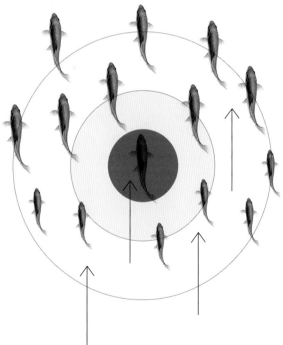

Dr Jason Hill of Dynamiq Engineering was our streamlining guru and he reckoned that dolphins have developed a couple of handy slipstreaming techniques. The way that dolphins behave in the wild is one of the closest things in nature to what we were trying to achieve.

Researchers in San Diego, USA, found that a dolphin calf slipstreams by its mother's side. This means that when dolphins are swimming together in a pod the youngsters that are not yet strong enough to swim as fast as the grown-ups can still keep up.

The mother pushes her way through the water, creating a 'bow wave' of higher-pressure water around her and her calf.

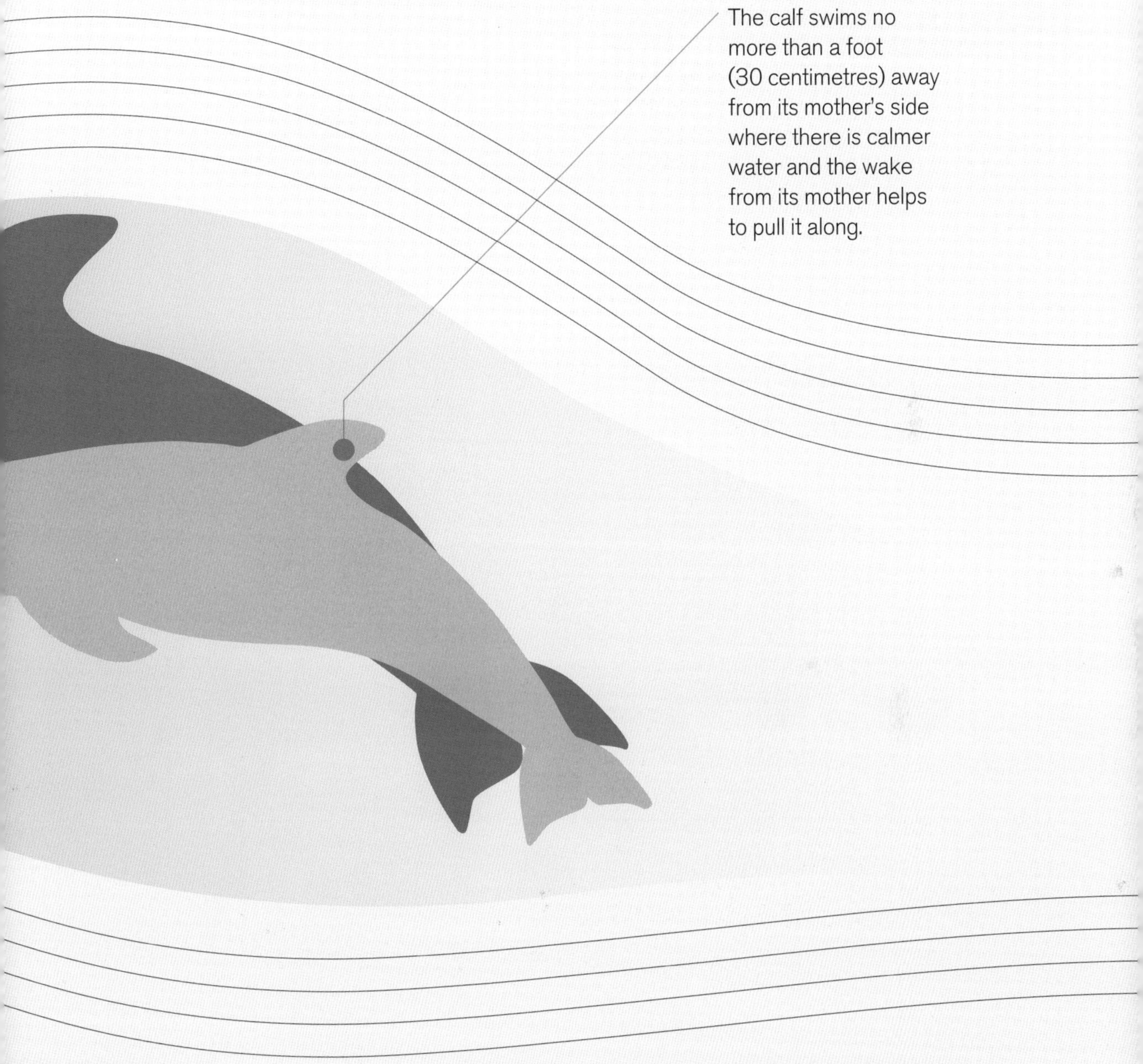

The calf swims no
more than a foot
(30 centimetres) away
from its mother's side
where there is calmer
water and the wake
from its mother helps
to pull it along.

Dolphins have also learned a cool trick
– bow-riding. When a ship pushes
forward through the water, it creates
a pressure wave at its bow. Dolphins
love to chase a ship and surf the pressure
wave. Speed, danger, fun? I like the way
those dolphins think!

Keep on Trucking

The Build Basics

You don't need a mind like Sir Isaac Newton's to work out that the two things I was going to need in order to break the British and Commonwealth record were a bike that could go pretty fast and something even faster to ride it behind.

WHEN the record had been set on the M42, the motor pace vehicle was a Rover SD1 car, although it was no ordinary Rover. The executive saloon built at British Leyland's Solihull factory was a big, four-door car with a hatchback, more used to being driven by managing directors and doctors than racing drivers, but Tom Walkinshaw Racing had enjoyed huge success with it in the British Touring Car Championship. In racing guise the car was capable of 160 mph, and it was one of these beasts that was used as the motor pace vehicle.

I fancied something altogether bigger; something that would give me the biggest slipstream 'pocket' possible; something that I was a good deal more familiar with than a saloon racer. A truck. Normally, the kind of trucks that I work on day-in, day-out in the workshop don't do more than 60 mph – that's the limit they have to stick to on a British motorway – but I needed something that could do twice that speed. That's where an amazing truck driver called Dave Jenkins came in. Jenkins Motorsport is a family business, and their business is racing trucks. We arranged to meet up with Dave at Bruntingthorpe Proving Ground near Lutterworth in Leicestershire. Bruntingthorpe, formerly RAF Bruntingthorpe, was and RAF base during the Second

Previous page: Chatting with Dave Jenkins under the nose of a retired Jumbo Jet at Bruntingthorpe.

Above: Dave shows that it's not only Formula One cars that can burn doughnuts on the track!

World War and a United States Air Force bomber base during the early years of the Cold War. Although no longer a military base, Bruntingthorpe is home to a museum collection of Cold War aircraft, including

two Lightning jet fighters that are being restored and maintained by the Lightning Preservation Group. In their heyday these British jets could do 1,300 mph – I doubt if I'd ever be able to catch one of them on my bike! Bruntingthorpe is also used as a test track by various car and tyre manufacturers because it has a two-mile-long concrete runway that is perfect for high-speed runs. It was on this runway circuit that Dave offered to show us what his truck could do. As you probably know, I'm no stranger to trucks, and

I know a bit about what these lads in their racing rigs get up to, but this was the first time I had got really 'up close and personal' with one of these beasts – and I'm talking about the truck here, not Dave. To most folk, the truck would look pretty much like an ordinary tractor unit. It has a cab where the driver and his mate sit and behind that is the flat 'deck' chassis with the 'fifth wheel' coupling where the trailer unit would normally hook up. That bit is completely fake. You can't hook a trailer up to Dave's truck, but if you could, you could scare the living

Above: My view of the truck – the first outing at Bruntingthorpe on the bike.

daylights out of Eddie Stobart's boys on the motorway, because this truck is seriously fast. It looks like a truck in the way that a rally car looks like the sort of five-door hatchback your granny takes to Sainsbury's to do her shopping.

In the cab, just like on the inside of a rally car or saloon racer, all of the creature comforts a driver enjoys have been stripped out. A normal truck has a driver's seat the size of an armchair with its own suspension and infinite adjustments for height and rake. Dave's seat is a simple bucket racing seat with a five-point racing harness. The entire dashboard is missing, replaced by gauges to show speed, revs, turbo boost and temperatures – the things Dave needs to keep an eye on when he's racing.

There's not a hint of carpet or ergonomic fittings – it's all bare metal, rivets, wiring loom and bolt heads. There aren't normally even any side windows in the thing when it is racing, just plastic mesh to stop bits of debris that have fallen off other trucks flying in to hitch a lift in the cab.

Again, like a rally car, the fairings, spoilers and aerodynamic aids on the truck are custom made, although race rules are imposed to make sure that the trucks do look as much as possible like the sort of units you will see on the road. Dave's MAN TGA truck has a six-cylinder, 12-litre turbocharged engine mated to a 16-speed gearbox. That sounds pretty much like a normal truck, too, but the engine in a regular MAN truck produces about 440 horsepower. Race tuned and with an enlarged turbo, Dave's produces 1,050 horsepower. To give you an idea what that means, this racing engine produces ten times as much power as an average small car. When I asked how fast it could go, Dave just shrugged and said, 'We can hit 130 mph without too much problem.'

When I asked how fast it could go, Dave just shrugged and said, 'We can hit 130 mph without too much problem.'

When I grinned at him and said 'No way!' he smiled and told me to get in. What followed was, for me, almost beyond belief. Dave put the MAN through its paces, casually chatting away to me as he slid the thing round corners sideways, tyres screaming and smoking. I thought we were about to go end-over-end at any moment but Dave always had the rig perfectly balanced on the throttle and the brakes and after just one lap I had 100%

confidence in what he was doing, so I sat back and enjoyed the white-knuckle ride of my life. Then, back on the starting line with Dave having sorted out a few minor niggles that were annoying him, he let me have a go. Dave sat in the passenger's bucket seat and urged me on, telling me where to break and when to give it some welly. I could never hope to post lap times as good as Dave's but we did make 120 mph with me behind the wheel, by which time I was totally convinced that Dave and his truck were what we needed to break the record.

I had my bike with me in the back of my van, so we decided to have a bash to see how fast we could go with me pedalling behind the truck. Dave rumbled forward on the runway, slowly building up speed, and I pedalled on behind as best I could, but ultimately we were disappointed. I couldn't get above about 37 mph (60 km/h) and I know I can do better than that on my own out on the open road – so what were we doing wrong?

Above: The truck's view of me – Dave could keep an eye on me using a screen on his instrument panel and a camera mounted on the back of the cab.

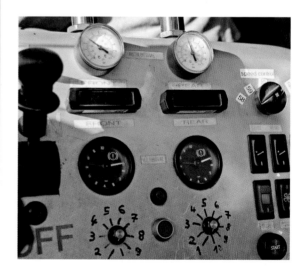

Above: The racing truck's dashboard was built purely for function rather than to look pretty – not the sort of truck interior I'm used to dealing with at all.

Getting the Slipstream Right

Aerodynamics expert Jason Hill was just the man to explain why I wasn't able to get above 37 mph behind the truck, no matter how hard I pedalled.

WHEN I expected that the truck in its racing form would provide me with a beautiful slipstream effect, Jason explained that the air being pushed aside in all directions – up, down and to the sides – by the front of the truck cab then collapses back in behind.

Normally this would create not only a pocket of still air for me to ride in but the air coming in behind would also give me a bit of a push – all good things. Unfortunately, because the bed of the truck, where the engine sits and the trailer would normally hook up, is an open framework of chassis and running gear, turbulent air was flowing up from below the cab as well as straight through underneath, probably serving to hold me back.

The main problem, though, was that the cab was the thing providing the slipstream and the back of the cab was too far ahead of me. The air collapsing in behind the cab was creating that vital 'pocket' somewhere above the bed and all I was getting was a wash of turbulent air which, again, was more of a hindrance than a help. What we needed, I thought, was to close off the gaps in the chassis and make the whole thing more aerodynamic. Jason disagreed. 'What we need,' he said, 'is for the truck to be about as aerodynamic as a brick. We want square sides, a flat floor and a flat rear end that you can ride as close to as possible.'

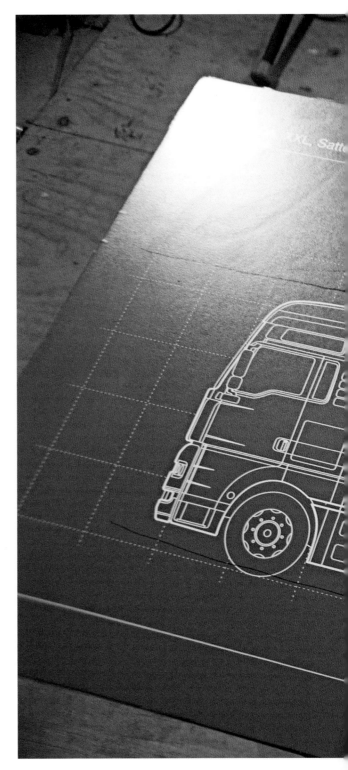

Previous page: Jason Hill roughs out a few sketches to show how the air will flow around the truck.

Above: The flat screen fairing was the most effective way of creating the slipstream pocket.

Riding behind a 'brick' the air it pushed aside would collapse behind me, pushing me along, and I would have that vital slipstream pocket to pedal in.

Jason showed me four different computer-generated models of how the slipstream behind the truck would work using different kinds of fairings.

With the standard truck, the area of dead air that I wanted to be in was too far ahead of me and I was, instead, cycling though an area of turbulence that was actually making things more difficult for me. The second scenario showed how it would work with a totally square truck, the roof extended right to the back and a flat rear end and sides extending down almost to the ground – the 'brick' that

Jason described earlier. This provided a good slipstream envelope for me to ride in; pretty much what we were after.

The only problem might be that the screen would create so much drag for the truck that it wouldn't be able to go fast enough.

Another possibility was to use a shed-type canopy, a bit like the fairing that Mile-a-Minute Murphy had on the back of his steam train. This would create a slightly better bubble but, at the sort of speed we were talking about, any slight error or bump on the ground could take me into the side walls without any chance of me being able to recover control.

The fourth concept was a far simpler affair. Basically, it was a flat screen attached to the

Above: Dave added a shelf at the bottom of the fairing to stop debris flying up at me.

back of the truck that would extend from roof level to ground level. The area of the truck between the cab and the screen would remain open. Using this fairing, the air would be parted by the truck cab, collapse in behind it and then be blasted out of the way again, creating the biggest slipstream envelope of all for me to work in. That's the one that Jason recommended we go for. The only problem might be that the screen would create so much drag for the truck that it wouldn't be able to go fast enough. Dave Jenkins reckoned that his truck would be able to cope, so we got into his workshop and rolled up our sleeves to start building the framework to support the screen.

MIG Welding the Fairing

We did, of course, have a lot of help from the team at Jenkins Motorsport in building the fairing and from Jason Hill in working out how best to support something that looked like an advertising hoarding that would be travelling at over 100 mph.

The steel sections that made up the framework were MIG welded, an arc welding process. MIG stands for Metal Inert Gas and it uses a particular type of welding kit. MIG welding works by supplying an electrical current that arcs between the welding torch and the metal pieces you are trying to join. It's like harnessing the power of a bolt of lightning. The heat that is created, up to 20,000° Celsius – many times hotter than the surface of the sun – melts the two metal surfaces at the spot where you want them to join. The molten metal fuses together as it quickly solidifies again and the two pieces become one.

The electrode from which the arc is emitted also melts, helping to fill any tiny unwanted deformities in the weld, and it is fed through the welding gun as a long piece of wire made from a metal that is compatible with whatever metals you are welding. That accounts for the metal part. The inert gas argon is commonly used, doesn't burn or react with the molten metal and is sprayed onto the metal as the weld is made to provide a protective barrier that prevents any other gases or substances in the atmosphere from contaminating, possibly weakening, the weld. MIG welding is a fast and efficient process that produces solid, strong welds, ideal for supporting a huge flat board against a 'wind' of more than 100 mph.

The framework was bolted to the chassis of Dave's truck, with Jason suggesting a couple of extra mounting points where it might need to be strengthened. Then the board was bolted to the frame and the fairing was ready to be tested. In the meantime, I had to sort out the other essential piece of kit – a bike capable of taking me faster than I'd ever pedalled before!

Above: At Pendine Sands I had to cycle through a cloud of grit behind the truck, now painted black.

Building a Record Breaker

The kind of bike that I needed wasn't the sort of thing that you could pick up in the average high street cycle shop.

NOTHING you could buy in the shops would do the job, and when I went to visit Brian Rourke at Rourke Cycles in Stoke on Trent I found out why.

Brian has been building bespoke bikes for discerning customers for the last 35 years and he uses all of his vast experience (he was a competitive road racer for 25 years and still does 150 miles a week at the age of 70) to make sure that people who ride bicycles with Rourke frames have the best-fitting bike that money can buy. He had me sit on a 'template' bike that he was able to adjust in all sorts of ways, all to make sure that, when I was sitting with my bum in the saddle, my hands and feet would be in the right place to ensure that my whole posture was geared to help produce maximum power when I pushed the pedals.

He chatted constantly, had me get off and on the bike, told me to pedal backwards and generally had a bit of a laugh until he finally said, 'There – now you're properly relaxed. You were a bit uptight when you came in, and what a difference it's made to the way

Top: The top and bottom chain rings, made by the lads at Hope Technology in Lancashire, that would allow me to maximise my pedal power.

Bottom: Front wheel resting neatly in the fork – the bike was beautifully put together.

you're sitting.' He was right, of course. Brian had put me at my ease and found the perfect arrangement of frame tube angles and lengths for my build. The difference between the way he had the 'template' bike set up to the way I thought it ought to be when we started had meant adding a few millimetres here and a couple of centimetres there, and the comparison was dramatic. The bike felt fantastic, but this was just a template to measure what I needed. The real bike build was yet to come.

The frame measurements that Brian had taken with the able assistance of Gareth, who's learned more about bikes while working with Brian than I will ever know, were passed to Brian's son, Jason, who builds the famous Rourke frames. Using a jig to hold everything in place, Jason showed me how he puts one of these masterpieces together. For Jason, the most important thing was to make sure that every angle was precise, every measurement unfailingly accurate and every weld absolutely straight. He was more worried than I was about the record attempt. In fact, he said he would rather be riding the bike than building it, so concerned was he that the bike would perform flawlessly. At those sorts of speeds, you see, if the bike is not perfectly aligned the frame can flex or wobble – and I would be left picking my teeth out of my nose . . . again.

Top: I was proud to have my name on such a fantastic machine.

Bottom: From an arty angle this chain could almost be part of any average bike . . .

TIG Welding the Bike Frame

Jason used steel tubes for the frame – specialist tubing made in Birmingham by a company called Reynolds – because he reckons British is best and steel gives him the best results. It is stronger and stiffer than aluminium or titanium but more supple than carbon fibre, so it absorbs bumps better.

The tubes were TIG welded, which is a form of arc welding like MIG welding but the electrode is made of tungsten (TIG is Tungsten Inert Gas) and doesn't melt into the weld. Instead, the welder feeds metal into the weld from a rod held in his spare hand. This is a more laborious form of welding that is used for jobs that require maximum precision.

The rest of the bike build involved sourcing the right kind of tyres, and Jason took advice from the Continental company. The kind of tyres used by road racers would be too skinny for us. We really needed something a little wider that would give me more traction, better grip. The wheels were to be fairly standard, if high-quality-items but it was the gearing that was key to helping me break the record. To the untrained eye, the rest of my 100 mph bike might not look like anything too much out of the ordinary, but the gears were always going to look different.

Right: The incredible Rourke bike on a stand to try to keep the sand out before we really got going.

Getting into Gear

Gears, in the simplest terms, are a way of multiplying the effort your legs make.

IF YOU had a cog on the bottom crank, the cog where you pedal, that was the same size as the cog on the rear wheel, then one turn of the pedal would cause the rear wheel to turn once. One turn equals one turn. If you make the front cog twice as big as the rear cog, then one pedal turn equals two turns of the rear wheel. The smaller cog has to turn faster in order to keep up, meaning that the wheel turns faster and your speed increases.

To get me to somewhere between 110 and 111 mph, the cog at the bottom crank would have to be so big that I wouldn't have the strength to turn it, even if it could actually be fitted onto Jason's frame without it dragging on the ground! The answer was to have two bottom cranks, massively multiplying the gear ratio. I reckoned that most people who have bikes understand how having 21 gears can make you go faster than if you only have 18, but there was no sensible way to put a number on what gear I would actually be in. The best way to describe it is to say that it was a 466-inch gear. That means that for one turn of the pedals I would travel 466 inches across the ground. That is an incredible 38 feet 10 inches (11.84 metres) every time I turned a pedal through a full revolution.

The bike had a fixed rear wheel. No free-wheeling would be possible; when the wheels turned, my feet, fixed in the pedals, would be turning, too. For convenience, Jason did fit

Left: One of the large bottom gears that would help deliver the 466-inch gear.

Above: The front wheel disc brake – safe enough if I used it wisely.

Following page: The bike was ready for the challenge, but was I?

a disc brake, at first intending it only to be on the bike when he took it out to test it. Those of you who have pulled on the front brakes and gone over the handlebars of your bike will be shaking your heads while reading this, but if you apply a brake like that properly and don't lock the wheel, it can be a very useful thing to scrub some speed when you need to slow down a bit. Jason used it when he took the bike out and tested it on a steep descent. He needed a hill because with the 466-inch gear you can't actually start pedalling, you need a tow or an assist to get going. Jason got going to about 60 mph and reckoned that the bike was every inch as good as he could have hoped.

Now I had the truck as a pace vehicle and a bike capable of keeping up with it, the only thing that needed to be made ready for the record attempt was yours truly. Was I actually capable of delivering enough raw power to keep up with Dave's truck once the speed really started to mount?

Feeling the Burn
Getting up to Speed

Getting to over 100 mph on a bike with an engine isn't too difficult if your engine has enough power but on a pushbike the only engine is yours truly – so the question was, did I have the power?

TO FIND out we visited Loughborough University, a world leader in sports technology research and home to the Sports Science Service where performance data for athletes like Mo Farrar and Victoria Pendleton was analysed. I was in good hands there, with Dr Rhona Pearce and Sarah Moseley putting me through my paces.

I rode a high performance ergonometer – a fancy exercise bike that could measure my power output and general performance. It was here that I learned about aerobic and anaerobic energy and how my bike's engine – me – needed the right kind of fuel to produce the power that would take me to 120 mph.

Basically, the energy you need to generate in order to make your muscles work is generated by glycogen that is stored in the muscles. The glycogen breaks down to form a sugar called glucose that combines with oxygen in your bloodstream, which comes from the air that you breathe, to create carbon dioxide (which you breathe out) and water, releasing energy in the process. When your body is working at about 65 per cent maximum performance, you can suck in enough air to keep that chemical reaction working efficiently. Glycogen levels in the muscles will reduce but glucose will be topped up as your heart pumps blood to the muscles, the blood carrying both oxygen and

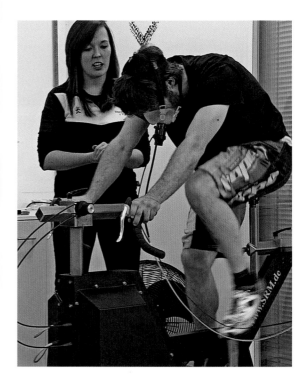

Above: Sarah Moseley urges me on to reach peak power output on the ergonometer at Loughborough University.

glucose. The glucose comes from fat stores, your converting fat more quickly to keep up with the increased demand. That's why moderate exercise is so good for shedding a few pounds.

Aerobic exercise is when you are working within your comfort zone and the oxygen

 **Carbon Dioxide** + **Water** +  **High Energy**

supply can keep up with the sugar supply, allowing an efficient chemical reaction. Anerobic exercise is when you are forcing your muscles to work at maximum capacity and you can't supply enough oxygen. It produces just 5 per cent as much energy as aerobic exercise as glucose is 'burned' inefficiently. It's a bit like having unused fuel coming out the exhaust pipe of your car only in this case it causes a build-up of lactate in the muscles. This starts to make life very difficult. First you feel a burning in the muscles and then, if you keep hard at it, you will start to feel sick as the lactate accumulates in your bloodstream – then you will collapse in a heap and throw up.

I didn't quite get to the throwing up stage on the ergometer but I was definitely starting to feel the burn and puffing like an old steam engine. There's a time and a place for being stubborn, and this is it. When your legs are swearing at you, you just have to keep on keeping on. Rhona and Sarah were cheering me on to hit my peak power output but ultimately the tests showed that I wasn't quite there. I wasn't producing the sustained power that would be needed to hit 120 mph. I could produce good levels of power in short bursts – the kind of thing I do ploughing through mud or up a steep rise on my mountain bike – but even though I was rated at a level twice as good as an average cyclist, it still wasn't enough.

The only way to delay the onset of the anerobic shut-down is through high intensity training, getting your body used to working harder so that you can keep oxygen/glucose energy conversion system working at peak efficiency for longer. I've never been one to shy away from hard work, so I was prepared to get stuck into some proper training, but I'm more than willing to take a bit of advice from those who know best and Laura Trott was just the girl.

 **Glucose** >  **Lactic Acid** +  **Low Energy**

The Laura Trott Effect

I felt a bit guilty about hauling Olympic gold medallist Laura Trott OBE along to a wet and miserable airfield in the middle of the night, but I needn't have worried, though. Laura is a tough competitor.

BORN prematurely with a collapsed lung, Laura has suffered from asthma all of her life and also has a problem with acid reflux. The reflux condition causes her to vomit after heavy exercise – the poor lass throws up after most training sessions and races even without the lactate overload that Rhona and Sarah explained to me at Loughbrough Uni. Despite all of that, Laura never seems to stop smiling and giggling. She's a lovely lass and, at just 21 years old, she has won more cycle races than you can shake a stick at, as well as two gold medals in the 2012 Olympics.

Laura is, of course, an expert in slipstreaming. Riding with her team-mates they tuck in behind one another, letting the leader create the slipstream that allows the others to use up to 30% less energy. The team each takes a turn as leader and they thunder round the velodrome. It was an aerodrome rather than a velodrome where Laura put me through my paces – Humberside Airport to be precise. They kindly agreed to let us use the runway at night once it was closed to air traffic and we could have a good, long, straight run to see what speed we could reach. Wearing skin-tight lycra and feeling less manly than I have ever done in my entire life, I tried a few high-speed runs on my own bike with Laura urging me on, yelling encouragement from the back of a truck driving

Above: The wet and windy conditions were far from perfect but I had an airport runway and Laura Trott all to myself.

alongside. In the conditions, I couldn't get much above 30 mph. Then we tried it together, with me slipstreaming behind Laura. Even in the awful weather that we had that night I got up to 36 mph – a 20% increase in speed.

Laura later paid me a visit at home to help out with fitness training. I thought I had been working hard but she had me doing interval training on a stationary bike, running on rollers. She timed me riding for 20 seconds hard followed by 20 seconds flat out, and we did that six times. By the end I was ready to drop and that was when Laura admitted that after most training sessions she has pushed herself so hard that she's sick, her reflux condition and the anaerobic effect combining to produce an unpleasant result.

Right: Even with Laura's encouragement, I couldn't get above 30 mph on my own.

The Record Holder

There was another Olympian that I simply had to talk to before I went any further with the record attempt – Dave Le Grys.

DAVE is a cycling legend. He represented Britain at the Montreal Olympics in 1976 and was back in Canada for the Commonwealth Games in Alberta in 1978, where he won silver along with partner Trevor Gadd in the Men's Tandem event but also crashed spectacularly when their front tyre blew at high speed. Dave broke his back and had to be air-lifted to hospital. Needless to say, he was back cycling again as soon as he was able, turning professional and going on to win a string of national and world titles, as well as becoming a hugely respected coach. He's also run the London Marathon five times and, at 57, is still competing in veterans events. For me, however, Dave's most important achievement was that it was him who rode the bike behind the Rover on the M42 in 1986. Dave Le Grys was the British and Commonwealth cycle speed record holder.

> Fear can be fun? Of course it can! It's one of the things that gives you a competitive edge and lets you know that you're still alive.

I was a bit nervous about going to meet Dave. After all, he might not take kindly to someone coming along determined to break his record. I needn't have worried – Dave couldn't have been more helpful. He explained how he had used

Above: Dave Le Grys was full of encouragement and didn't mind me trying to break his record at all.

a bike that was more of a road racing machine with skinny tyres but it used the same gearing system that we were to use, with two bottom brackets to multiply the real wheel rotations in relation to the pedal rotations. His record run was one of three that they made on the M42 the day before it opened, with them changing the bike gears to go faster on each run and altering the fairing that was fitted to the back of the pace car. It was all done under pressure as well, with the weather closing in, more wind than they would have liked and rain on the way. He made 110 mph on his third run, but on the fourth run he was to be going for 135 mph! Unfortunately for him, the rain came bucketing down and he was never able to make his fourth pass.

Dave is a man who deals with the facts, and I like that, because he wasn't afraid to admit that hitting 110 mph behind a saloon racing car 'scared the living hell out of me, but it was good fun'. Fear can be fun? Of course it can! It's one of the things that gives you a competitive edge

Above: Dave thundering along behind the racing Rover on the M42 in 1986.

Dave reckoned that 'you've got to
be kind of nuts to do it' and seemed
to think I was well qualified.

and lets you know that you're still alive. When it comes to riding a push bike at over 100 mph, Dave reckoned that 'you've got to be kind of nuts to do it' and he seemed to think I was well qualified . . .

When I asked him if he was bothered that we were out to break his record, Dave simply said, 'Not at all. I encourage you to go for it. You've got good people behind you. You can do it.' Dave inspired me with confidence. He was

roughly the same age as me when he set the record and, having just finished a racing season, he was fit as a butcher's dog. My basic fitness is pretty good but I knew I had to work hard to make sure I was spot on for the attempt. I wasn't about to let everyone down by not putting in the graft on the fitness front. Dave spent six weeks getting himself ready to set the record on the M42 and I had about the same to get myself ready to break it.

The Moment of Truth

With the truck ready, the bike ready and me just about ready, what we really had to do was get everyone together for a test session.

WE ALL assembled back at Bruntingthorpe where Dave Jenkins and his lads had the truck in top condition with the fairing looking good, while the Rourke team had the bike looking like a dream machine. The fairing – actually quite similar to the 'shield' used by Letourner all those years ago – now had a brake bar attached, the idea being that, when the truck slowed down, a vertical post mounted on the front of the bike would nudge the horizontal bar sticking out from the fairing to help slow me down. The bike also still had its front disc brake which, because it weighed so little, we had decided to keep.

I had been getting used to riding a fixed wheel bike by using one supplied by the Rourke lads to ride to work every day, instead of using my Cotic. It helped me to get my technique right as I needed to be as smooth as possible when pushing the pedals. If you watch road racers at an event like the Tour de France, when they are sitting in the saddle travelling at speed their leg movements are really fluid, not jerky or snatched. This makes sure that they are delivering maximum power most efficiently to the pedals. Some of them actually train by slipstreaming behind pace cars to perfect their technique for racing. Not many of them will have topped 100 mph, though! For trying out the bike behind the truck, I climbed into an old set of racing leathers. Dave Le Grys had had leathers specially made in London for his

Above: After the test session at Bruntingthorpe we were ready to go for the record.

record run. The leathers had to allow him to move, so needed to be custom tailored, but my old leathers gave me all the movement I needed. The most important thing was that, if I was to come off the bike at over 100 mph, as Dave put it, 'Unless you hit anything solid, you will slide.' I certainly know that feeling from having come off racing motorbikes. Sliding along the ground slows you down and, providing you're not tumbling tip over tail, brings you to a halt without crunching too many bones. The leathers protect your skin as much as possible. Wearing cycling lycra, the friction involved in sliding along at those speeds would skin you alive. I also wore a full-face racing helmet.

The plan was for the truck to tow me up to around 60 mph, at which point the tow cable would be released and I would be on my own. We tried it all out and it all appeared to work perfectly, so there was nothing to stop us having a go at a high-speed run there and then, was there?

We set off down the runway, Dave building up speed in the truck as planned and my legs turning faster and faster on the fixed wheel. Then the cable was released and I pumped my legs harder than ever before, concentrating on keeping myself running straight and true 'in the zone' behind the truck. It was going well up to the point where I had a bit of a wobble when the front wheel was taken sideways by a slight ridge on the runway. Anyone who's ever ridden a bike knows what it feels like when your front wheel is taken away from you by a crack in the road, a drain or a tramline. It gives you a bit of a scare until you pull it back again. Imagine what that feels like at the kind of speed we were doing. For a second I forgot to pedal and then had to unclip one of my feet and was struggling to stay upright. Dave, who could see me on a monitor screen inside the truck cab, immediately started to slow down and we came to a halt with me still in one piece.

Dave jumped out the cab and ran round to see how I was, and I just couldn't stop grinning. That's what speed is all about for me. That's why I love going fast – because you know that it could all go horribly wrong and there comes a moment when you are out there on the edge. I love those moments. Money can't buy them.

My grin just got wider when Dave told me that we had done 111.7 mph. We had broken Dave Le Grys's record but not by enough to shout it from the rooftops. We needed to go much faster, but looking at the length of runway ahead of us by the time we had come to a standstill, it was clear that we didn't have much space left at all. Dave Le Grys had used the M42 because they didn't think they could get up to speed on a runway or a race track, and he'd been spot on. Bruntingthorpe had been great for us so far, but it we were going to go faster we were going to need a longer track.

Top: The cable that towed me along to almost 60 mph before being released from the truck.

Bottom: The small gear that works with the two large gears to crank up the speed.

Going for the Record

Pendine Sands on Carmarthen Bay in Wales is a beach seven miles long which is famous for being used as a racing and record-breaking venue.

YOU would think that nobody goes cycling on a beach. Your wheels sink into the sand, your chain gets clogged up and it all turns into a bit of a nightmare. That's not the way it works at Pendine Sands – or so we thought.

In the 1920s the Welsh TT motorcycle races were staged here and in 1924 Malcolm Campbell (he wasn't *Sir* Malcolm until 1931) brought his Blue Bird car to Pendine to set a World Land Speed Record of 146.16 mph. Pendine, you see, is no ordinary beach. When the tide goes out the sand dries so hard and flat that you could drive a tractor over it without making a dent. When Campbell set his record, there was no stretch of road or race track in the UK that was as long, straight and flat as Pendine Sands.

Previous page: I was concentrating so hard on doing my job that I never really noticed the helicopter.

Top: The TV crew's chopper gets a birds-eye view.

Middle: Setting out the track.

Bottom: My cycle shoes kept my feet clipped onto the pedals, whatever speed I was doing.

Far right: Preparing the bike for its first run at Pendine Sands.

110 mph

Set by Dave Le Grys in 1986

The whole team came together for the trip to the seaside, also in attendance were Mike Broadbent from Racelogic whose high-tech equipment would be used to record our speed and Graham Bristow, General Secretary of the British Pacing Association, who would verify the speed Graham logged to keep everything official and watertight.

The weather forecast had been for showers but it turned out to be bright sunshine – pretty good apart from the 20 mph breeze that was blowing. High tide was before dawn at around 4.30 am and we had to wait until the tide had gone out, not just to expose the sand but to let it pack firm enough to create the surface that we needed. Of course, the tide would eventually come back in again, the water would rise up through the sand and the surface would become unstable. Just as Dave Le Grys had had a window of opportunity before the rain closed in, we had our six-hour window when the surface would be good enough between tides. That was the plan, anyway.

The stretch of beach we were going to use was more than two and a half miles long, which should easily have been long enough for us, but when Dave Jenkins took the truck out to get used to driving at speed on the sand we could all see straight away that Pendine was not going to be the ideal surface for our record run. When put to the test, the sand was not as rock hard as we had expected. It moved. That gave Dave a bit of a problem in keeping the truck going in a straight line and, compared with the concrete at Bruntingthorpe, the sand wasn't giving him the kind of traction he wanted, meaning that he could only make 118 mph. The softer surface was soaking up some of the truck's power. Worse still, I could expect it to do the same to me.

The other thing that was obvious to everyone was that Dave was dislodging loose, dry, surface sand that was forming a cloud behind the truck. Dave fitted baffles at the bottom of the fairing as well as filling in the space between the stop bar and the fairing to try to prevent sand from flying up at me from below the truck. Jason Hill reckoned that would help, but he was more concerned about the way that loose sand was flying around behind the truck. There were also worries about debris on the course, including scraps of driftwood and dead jellyfish. Anything we could see could be cleared out of the way, but if there was something just below the surface that was flung up by the truck – well, nobody wants to be hit in the head with a dead jellyfish at 100 mph, do they?

Finally, everybody was ready for the first run, and we set off. As our speed built up, things started to get pretty hairy behind the truck. Sand was flying everywhere. I felt like I was being shot blasted and, while I really wanted to try to keep myself between one and two metres behind the truck, using taped markings on the fairing to keep me slightly off centre in order to take the breeze into account, visibility was so bad that if I dropped back as much as one metre I couldn't see the marks. Any more than that and I could barely see the truck. Breathing wasn't easy either. It felt like my tonsils were being sandpapered. Nevertheless, on that first run we made it to 102 mph.

Before the second run, Dave took the truck down the course again, the fairing was checked to make sure it was all okay and me and the bike

---

Following page: Getting up to speed before I really had to hit my peak power output.

Right: Not your usual Pendine car park customer!

had the sand shaken out of us. Having done the first run on racing slicks, the truck was fitted with different tyres to try to give Dave more grip, the bike was given a bigger gear, then we set off again. By now the sun, the wind and the truck had loosened the surface sand to the extent that the second run was even worse than the first. The air flow around the truck and the fairing was working exactly as Jason Hill had predicted, with the air that had been pushed out of the way collapsing back in behind the truck and being sucked in to the area of low pressure. The trouble was, it was bringing sand with it. I was being blasted from both sides and the rear, although the new baffles on the truck and fairing were minimising the stuff coming at me head on.

Below: Attaching the tow cable. We filled in the stop bar to make a kind of shelf. I could have had a mug of tea on there ...

Top right: Close to the truck, still on the tow cable.

Bottom right: Dropping back slightly once the cable was released – more speed, please, legs!

Visibility was worse than ever. My visor was steaming up but I couldn't raise it because I would get sand straight in my eyes and be able to see nothing at all. I was struggling to breathe and, worst of all, the bike was not entirely stable. I wasn't sinking into the surface as you would if you tried cycling on a normal beach, but I was leaving a slight track, which meant that I was wasting power, and I needed all the power I could generate. With the surface shifting ever so slightly, I was also feeling the bike wobble. It made my 'moment' at Bruntingthorpe seem like a stroll in the park. Altogether, it was a pretty horrific experience, but there was no way I was going to quit. We finished the second run – 112.9 mph.

Altogether, it was a pretty horrific experience, but there was no way I was going to quit.

I felt utterly knackered, but I knew that if I had a chance to catch my breath I would be able to give it another go. Dave was up for it as well and we probably had enough time to do it, but wiser heads said no. The conditions were deemed too dangerous. If I were to come off the bike, I would not slide along the surface like I have done in the past on concrete or tarmac. A knee, an elbow or my head would dig in and it would be pretty much like hitting a brick wall.

We had beaten the record, albeit not by as much as we had hoped and the frustrating thing was that we knew we could have done far better. The surface at Pendine had held us back but we had won through in the end. All we needed was a long stretch of smooth empty road – I wonder if the men at the transport ministry have got any plans to close the M42 again?

Human Powered Aircraft

Current record: 27.5 mph
Record holder: Holger Rochelt
Nationality: German
Record set: 1985

The Challenge

'This was going to test me more than any other physical challenge I had ever faced.'

I THINK everyone knows the story of Daedalus and Icarus. But it doesn't matter if you don't, because we will be coming back to those two. Suffice to say that when I came across a picture of these ancient Greek characters wearing their home-made wings on their arms, it reminded me of those blokes you used to see on telly, jumping off the end of the pier at Bognor hoping to fly. They all tended to fly like bricks, and that made me think that there surely must be a better way for a man to fly under his own steam. I then found out that there was, and if a man could fly using muscle power, then flying faster than anyone else was a challenge I fancied having a go at.

Getting off the ground under your own muscle power simply can't be done with your arms. You need to generate so much power that you have to use the biggest muscle groups, and that means bringing your legs into the game. You can't flap your legs like a bird's wings, of course – leg power means pedal power, but just how much power would we need to get me off the ground and what sort of flying machine would I have to use?

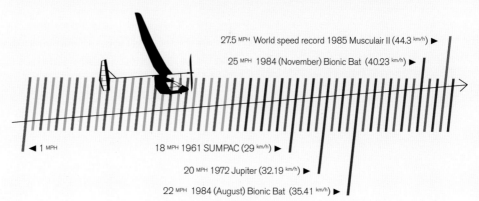

27.5 MPH World speed record 1985 Musculair II (44.3 km/h) ▶

25 MPH 1984 (November) Bionic Bat (40.23 km/h) ▶

◀ 1 MPH

18 MPH 1961 SUMPAC (29 km/h) ▶

20 MPH 1972 Jupiter (32.19 km/h) ▶

22 MPH 1984 (August) Bionic Bat (35.41 km/h) ▶

The solutions to those problems have been pondered over for years by people far cleverer than me, yet not all of them have managed to get a man in the air, and even those who have got their man off the ground haven't always managed to keep him there for very long! The aircraft that they have built to make their flying attempts in the past have often been weird and wonderful machines, but nowadays they all tend to have certain things in common. The materials used and the way that they are designed are often quite similar – after all, the people who make them are trying to achieve the same thing and have much the same bank of knowledge to draw on. But even if the machines do look a bit alike, there are still small but important differences that stem from the way the designers have approached the problem of getting a man into the air and what they hoped to achieve once they'd got him airborne. Do they want him to fly fast or cover a huge distance? If you think about it, there's a heck of a difference between a supersonic jet fighter and a long-haul passenger jet.

One of the things that many of the successful human-powered aircraft (HPAs) have in common is that they are built in Britain. There's a long tradition of record-breaking HPAs in the UK, and I had to look to some of these pioneers to show me how it can be done and where my biggest problems would lie.

In order to follow what they were telling me, I had to swot up on a few basic principles of flight and find out what keeps an aeroplane in the air. An important factor in building bigger and faster aircraft has been the development of engines, but I wasn't to have the luxury of that sort of technology. I was going to have to rely on my own muscle power, and that was ultimately to test me more than any other physical challenge I had ever faced.

Below: A simple bicycle chain would be used on our HPA, running up from the rear wheel to turn the propeller.

Above: The Airglow HPA flew well but with the pilot reclined he couldn't transfer the power from his legs to the pedals as well as he could if he had been sitting in a more traditional cycling position, and power means speed.

Discovering the World of Human Powered Flight

People have been dreaming about flying for as long, I should think, as people have been having dreams.

T**HERE'S** definitely something symbolic in imagining yourself soaring off into the sky, leaving all your troubles behind you. We see birds leaping into the air and flying off whenever they think they're in danger, and we too think of flying as being a kind of escape. Being able to fly gives you freedom. That's certainly how Daedalus and Icarus saw it.

According to Greek legend, Daedalus got himself into a right pickle after doing a bit of work for King Minos on the island of Crete. A spell had been cast over Minos' wife that made her fall in love with a bull, and she had a bit of a fling with the horny devil, resulting in a baby boy that was half human and half bull. When the little lad grew into a big, raging bull, he became a proper handful, able to break out of any room where they locked him up. Minos employed Daedalus, an architect and inventor, to build a prison that was a maze of corridors – the labyrinth – that the bull-boy, known as the Minotaur, could never escape from. Daedalus' son, Icarus, worked with his dad to build the labyrinth and only they knew the secret of how to get in and out of the maze of tunnels without becoming hopelessly lost. To make sure that they never told anyone and that the Minotaur stayed hidden away forever, Minos then locked the pair of them in a tower. Escaping from the tower might not have been too tough a challenge for someone as smart as Daedalus, but getting off the island was another matter, as the King controlled all of the shipping and his spies were everywhere.

In his prison tower, Daedalus came to the conclusion that the only way to escape from Crete was to fly like a bird. He gathered feathers and created wings, binding the feathers together using wax. With the wings strapped to their arms, Daedalus and Icarus were able to fly like birds. Daedalus warned his son not to fly too close to the sun or the wax would melt, but Icarus got a bit carried away, soared too high and his wings fell apart. He plunged into the sea and drowned.

> The legend of Daedalus and Icarus has inspired countless people over the years to try to fly like birds, taking to the air under their own steam rather than with the help of any kind of engine.

The legend of Daedalus and Icarus has inspired countless people over the years to try to fly like birds, taking to the air under their own steam rather than with the help of any kind of engine. One of the earliest was an eleventh-century monk known as Eilmer of Malmesbury. Eilmer built himself a hang-glider and bravely flew it off the top of a tower at Malmesbury Abbey. He glided for a couple of hundred metres before he lost control and plummeted to the earth. The fall broke both of his legs and he was lame for the rest of his days, but Eilmer wasn't simply some crackpot monk. He had studied the flight of birds and the way that they used thermal currents, and he reckoned that his big mistake had been in not giving himself a tail for stability. He was working on that problem when his boss, the abbot, banned him from any more flying stunts. Eilmer is known as 'The Flying Monk'.

More than 400 years after Eilmer took to the skies above Wiltshire, Leonardo da Vinci began thinking about how a man might fly, and he designed various flying contraptions including a parachute, a kind of helicopter and a thing called an 'ornithopter'. The ornithopter was a man-powered flying machine that the pilot operated by using his hands and feet to push levers that would flap wings. It's unlikely that Leonardo ever built his ornithopter and, given that the materials available to him would have been limited – basically wood and canvas – it would probably have been too heavy to fly using only the pilot's muscle power. His parachute worked, though. In 2000, using Leonardo's design and fifteenth-century materials and tools, British skydiver Adrian Nicholas built the huge pyramid of wood and canvas. The parachute was lifted to 3,000 metres (10,000 feet) by a hot-air balloon, then released with Nicholas dangling beneath. He claimed it gave as smooth a ride as any modern parachute.

Gliding and parachuting are all very well, but they're not *powered* flight. The pilot is flying, and in control, but is not providing the power that will keep him up there. When Wilbur and Orville Wright made their first flight in 1903, helping us to understand how an aircraft could be flown and controlled, their aeroplane was powered, but by an engine. The first man to leave the ground in a flying machine powered purely by himself was French professional cyclist Gabriel Poulain.

Poulain was competing for a prize of 10,000 francs (worth about £400 at a time when most people in Britain were earning less than £3 per

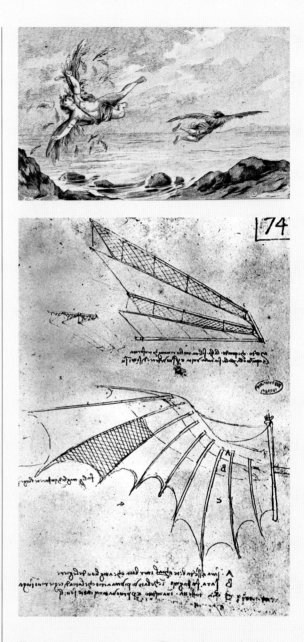

Top: Icarus came a cropper when his wings melted because he flew too close to the sun – not a problem I expected to have to deal with.

Bottom: Leonardo da Vinci designed a human powered hang-glider that experts believe would have flown, although one man would never have been strong enough to provide enough lift for take off.

Le Premier Homme-Volant

Sans le secours d'aucun moteur, par la seule force de ses muscles, Gabriel Poulain est parvenu le premier à faire un vol de plusieurs mètres. L'aviette dont il est l'inventeur a pu franchir un espace de 12 mètres à 1 mètre 20 au-dessus du sol.

Top: The Wright Brothers' *Wright Flyer* showing the distinctive forward wings and the pilot lying face down to create less air resistance and give better weight distribution.

Bottom: Front cover of the French newspaper *Le Petit Journal*, signed by Gabriel Poulain and showing him making his epic 12-metre glide.

week) offered by Robert Peugeot. The Peugeot family business included making cars and bicycles, so the competition was good publicity for them. The prize was for the first man to take off and fly under his own steam. The contest was first held in Paris in 1912 with hopeful competitors attaching wings to their bicycles to try to get airborne. Some just about got off the ground, but to win the big money prize you had to reach a height of at least one metre and cover a distance of at least ten metres.

The contest became an annual event and the winged bikes were known as *aviettes*. Some of the *aviettes* managed short hops and their pilots were awarded consolation prizes to encourage everyone to keep on trying, but it wasn't until 1921 that Gabriel Poulain took the cash, riding his biplane *aviette*. In the Bois de Boulogne, a huge public park in Paris, Poulain hurtled along the road leading to the Longchamps racecourse, heading for a large, square patch of white chalk on the ground. When he reached the chalk, by this time doing around 25 mph, he threw a lever to alter the angle of his wings and he took off. The tyre marks in the chalk showed that he stayed in the air for up to 12 metres on the runs that he made, and those watching judged that he had made it to more than a metre in height.

The *aviette* flight of Gabriel Poulain was a huge achievement, but it wasn't really human powered flight. He had managed a human-powered take-off, but once his wheels were off the ground he was no longer providing any kind of power. He had no propeller or any other kind of device to drive him through the air. What he did was to *glide* for 12 metres, and gliding is not powered flight. However, he had shown that it was possible for a human to provide the power needed to get airborne; the next challenge was to stay airborne.

Two years later, Dr Frederick Gerhardt, head of the Aeronautical Engineering Department and the University of Michigan, successfully flew one of the weirdest-looking aeroplanes ever seen. The Gerhardt Cycleplane had seven wings, stacked one on top of the other, like a biplane or triplane but with seven layers, making it nearly 15 feet tall. It didn't look like the sort of thing you could knock together in your tea break. It was a delicate machine, but the flimsy construction that was intended to make it as light as possible was also its downfall. In some comical footage, which you can find online, you can see it having a bit of a wobble as it's being pushed along the ground before the stacked wings all collapse inwards on to the fuselage.

It might have looked like something out of a Laurel and Hardy movie, but Gerhardt's aeroplane had actually flown. Pedal power turned a two-blade propeller in the aircraft's nose that pulled it along fast enough for it to make several short flights, but to get going fast enough for those flights it needed to be towed by a car. The only time that a human-powered take-off was attempted, they managed just a short hop of 20 feet at a height of only two feet.

The next real landmark event came in the 1930s when German inventor Engelbert Zaschka built a massive monoplane with a wingspan of around 66 feet (20 metres). It had a huge propeller and the pilot sat high off the ground, behind the propeller. The machine reportedly managed a brief flight of about 20 metres and is believed to have done so taking off under pedal power at Berlin's Tempelhof airport in 1934. During that decade far longer flights were made by other aircraft, such as the German HV-1 Mufli or the Italian Pedaliante, which stayed airborne for a full kilometre, but both the Mufli and the Pedaliante needed help from catapults

Top: Hopeful *aviette* flyer Paul Didier managed to glide about 5 metres on his flying bike in 1912.

Middle: The Gerhardt Cycleplane at McCook Field air base in Ohio in 1923, shortly before it all collapsed in a heap.

Bottom: German inventor Engelbert Zaschka's monoplane in 1934 without any fabric covering on the wings or tail. He reportedly made an unauthenticated human-powered take-off and short flight at Berlin's Templehof airport.

or winch systems to get them off the ground. Like so many other things, human-powered flight was pretty much put on the back burner during the Second World War, with aviation experts concentrating on the war effort, but by the 1950s human-powered flight was a talking point once more and in 1959 the Royal Aeronautical Society (RAeS) formed its Man Powered Aircraft Group. The RAeS has been around since 1866 as an organisation devoted to all forms of flying in the UK, and the Man Powered Aircraft Group (now renamed the Human Powered Aircraft Group as there have been so many successful lady pilots) was given the job of monitoring design developments and attempts by pedalling pilots to get off the ground.

Now it really was 'game on', and the competition, previously only open to British entries, became international.

Also in 1959, inventor and industrialist Henry Kremer decided to support the RAeS in their efforts to re-ignite interest in human-powered flight. Originally from Latvia, Kremer had lived in England since he was a child and he knew a thing or two about aircraft that used lightweight construction techniques. Special laminated wood devised by Kremer was used in building the De Havilland Mosquito, known as 'The Wooden Wonder', which was one of the fastest military aircraft in the world when it went into service with the RAF during the Second World War.

Kremer now grabbed everyone's attention when, like Robert Peugeot, he offered a cash prize to whoever could navigate a figure-of-eight course, flying over a measuring pole with a height of 3 metres (10 feet) at the beginning and end. The prize was £5,000, which might not sound like a huge amount nowadays, but to give you an idea of how much the prize was worth, at that time you could buy a brand-new Mini car – launched in 1959 – for less than £500.

With serious money on offer, serious interest was taken in cracking Kremer's challenge. This meant coming up with a design for an aircraft that could actually get off the ground using only the power generated by the pilot. The first HPA to make an officially authenticated man-powered take-off, flight and landing was the SUMPAC (Southampton University Man Powered Aircraft) in 1961. The team had 35 failed flights under their belts before they finally got the thing off the ground, but once they did get airborne they managed a fair distance – 64 metres (70 yards) at a height of 1.8 metres (6 feet). Their best flight was 594 metres (650 yards), when they reached the giddy height of 4.6 metres (15 feet). It wasn't enough to scoop a Kremer prize, but the Southampton University students had shown that it was possible for a pilot to take off and stay in the air using pedal power. The SUMPAC was quickly followed by the Hatfield Puffin, designed and built by employees of the De Havilland Aircraft Company, who managed a flight of 908 metres (993 yards), a distance record that was to remain unbroken for over 10 years.

The aircraft that eventually took the distance record from the Puffin was the Jupiter, another British-designed, British-built aeroplane that managed 1,239 metres (1,354 yards) in June 1972, but still flying in a straight line. No one had yet managed to master the problem of keeping the aircraft in the air and executing controlled turns. Kremer duly increased his prize pot to no less than £50,000 for the figure-of-eight course. Now it really was 'game on', and the competition, previously only open to British entries, became international.

In January 1977 a Japanese team from Tokyo's Nihon University flew an HPA called Stork which managed 2,094 metres (2,290 yards) and covered most of a figure-of-eight before a wing tip clipped the ground, bringing the aircraft down. Around the same time Dr Paul B. MacCready, a former US Navy pilot and champion glider pilot with degrees in physics and aeronautics, led the group that designed and built Gossamer Condor 2, the aircraft that claimed the £50,000 Kremer prize in August 1977. Flown by cyclist and hang-gliding enthusiast Bryan Allen, the Condor sailed round a 2,172-metre (2,375-yard) figure-of-eight at a stately 11 mph above Minter Field airport in California.

With the £50,000 prize gone, Kremer and the RAeS set a new and seemingly impossible challenge – to fly an HPA across the English Channel. The new prize was £100,000. In June 1979 Bryan Allen was back in the saddle at the controls of the Gossamer Albatross, another aircraft from the MacCready stable, which he flew from England to France. The crossing was more than 22 miles (almost 36 km) and took nearly three hours. Flying at just 1.5 metres (5 feet) above the sea, Allen suffered cramps in his legs and became dehydrated when he ran out of water. With three miles to go, he could see the beach in France that he was aiming for but felt totally spent and decided to follow the procedure for abandoning the flight. He climbed a little higher in order that the aircraft could be hooked up to a pylon aboard a motor boat, which would then tow it to the beach to avoid having to ditch in the sea.

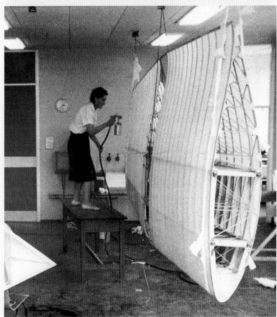

Top: The De Havilland Mosquito was one of the fastest combat aircraft in the world when it entered service in 1941 and was known as 'The Wooden Wonder' because its airframe and skin were made from wood.

Bottom: Working on the wings of the historic SUMPAC flying machine prior to its maiden flight.

Top: SUMPAC pilot Derek Piggott tries the cockpit for size with the rest of the team running through a few pre-flight checks.

Bottom: Employees from De Havilland's Hatfield factory put their woodworking skills to good use in building the Hatfield Puffin HPA and the Puffin II, pictured here in 1965.

Surprisingly, at the slightly increased height, Allen found the going easier and carried on to land on the beach.

The figure-of-eight had been flown and the English Channel had been conquered, so in 1983 the RAeS decided to set another challenge. No HPA had been known to fly at more than about 20 mph, so to encourage inventive engineers and designers to build faster HPAs, the challenge was to complete a 1.5 km (0.93 mile) course in less than three minutes. Henry Kremer again put up the prize money, this time offering £20,000 for the first to complete the challenge and £5,000 to anyone who could better the previous successful time by 5%.

A team from the Massachusetts Institute of Technology (MIT) began building the Monarch B in May 1983 and within a year they had it ready to go for the prize. After a number of setbacks, the Monarch B was flown around a course at the Lawrence G. Hanscom Field airport in Massachusetts in 2 minutes 54.7 seconds. That record stood for only a week before another MacCready design, Bionic Bat, knocked 11.4 seconds off the time, but Bionic Bat then lost the record a month later to Musculair I when it recorded a time almost 12 seconds faster than the Bat. Four months later the Bat reclaimed its record, but in October 1985 Musculair II appeared. The Musculair planes were fielded by a German father-and-son team, with Gunter Rochelt leading the design team and his 19-year-old son Holger pumping the pedals. This time they flew the triangle in 2 minutes and 2 seconds, setting a world record speed of 27.5 mph (44.3 km/h), and they shared the Kremer prize money pot between them.

If all of this suggests there are teams out there building HPAs purely to win cash prizes, then it's a bit misleading. The RAeS doesn't support competitions just so that a few flyers can make a bob or two. Likewise, people don't do it just for the money. Because of the amount of time that it takes to create an HPA, and the cost of the materials, getting a pilot into the air under his own steam is more of a labour of love. One of the aims of the RAeS is to promote HPA flying as a sport, and most of the participants at HPA events treat it as exactly that – a sport or hobby. Like the thousands of people who race cars and motorbikes, or sail yachts, or cycle, the HPA crews are enthusiasts using their skills and technical knowledge to try to do something pretty special. You have to admire their dedication and respect their achievements. Despite the records that have been set over the years, it's still quite something to design and build an HPA and get it into the air – more people have been into outer space than have flown an HPA. I may never make it into space, but I was determined to become an HPA pilot.

The competitive element, of course, is always there. Where's the fun if there's no edge? I reckoned that being at the controls of an HPA would be immense, but I couldn't help thinking about Musculair II. Surely we could manage a faster speed? I had pedalled a bike at 112 mph, after all, so getting up to around 30 mph on a bike with wings didn't seem completely out of the question, and it would be nice to think that a British team could design and build an HPA that could fly faster than the Germans, wouldn't it? The only snag was that I had never flown anything in my life. True, I had flown through the air when coming off a motorbike at a fair old speed, but you could never claim you were in control of that short flight and it seldom ends well! I knew nothing about piloting an aircraft, so before I went any further I needed to learn a few basics about flying ...

Top: The Gossamer Albatross had a wingspan of almost 30 metres (98 feet) yet weighed only 32 kilograms.

Middle: Gossamer Albatross leaving England at the start of a three-hour flight across the English Channel to France.

Bottom: The Musculair II by the German father-and-son team whose record I was going to try and beat.

Come Fly With Me

Why was I learning to fly a glider? Well gliders have many of the same characteristics as HPAs.

WHEN you look at an aircraft hangar with those huge sliding doors at the front, you would think that they must need a massive motor to crank them open. Not a bit of it. They slide aside so easily on their wheels that, just by putting my back into it, I was able to open the hangar doors where another Guy – Guy Westgate – had parked his gleaming, white two-seat glider. We were at Lee-on-Solent Airfield, formerly the Royal Naval Air Service Seaplane Training School. It also served as an RAF base and a Fleet Air Arm base known as HMS Daedalus – now where have we heard that name before? Guy's 'day job' is flying Boeing 747-400 airliners but he's been flying aerobatic gliders for over 20 years and has won the National Glider Aerobatic Championship eight times. He's an advanced aerobatic instructor and the best person I could ever hope to have as a flying instructor in a glider.

Learning to fly a glider would be excellent practice for the HPA. Our HPA would have to fly on the limited amount of power that I would be able to supply, and gliders fly without any on-board engine power at all. Gliders have massive wings – the wingspan of the glider Guy was to take me up in is 16.67 metres (almost 55 feet) – just like HPAs. Gliders are also built of lightweight materials and have extremely sensitive controls – completely different from the superjumbos Guy is used to flying, but very similar to HPAs.

Guy explained that even a short flight in a glider would give me a good understanding of some of the things that I would need to master in the HPA – keeping the wings level, for example, or avoiding 'stalling'. An aircraft will stall when its speed drops and the wing can no longer do its job of providing the 'lift' that keeps the whole thing airborne. We'll be coming back to exactly how wings work a little later, but I was about to get a practical demonstration of what happens in a 'stall' and it was immediately obvious why a 'stall' would scupper any HPA flight.

In the meantime, Guy had to get us airborne in the glider. We manhandled it out on to the runway and were then hooked up to a cable that would allow a small plane to tow us into the air. Guy and I sat one behind the other in the cockpit with me in the student's seat in front. We both had a set of instruments in front of us showing air speed, altitude, compass direction and suchlike, but one of the most important for me was the attitude indicator – yes, attitude, not altitude – also called the 'artificial horizon', that tells you whether you are nose up, nose down or dipping one wing lower than the other. My feet were on pedals that controlled the rudder and I had a joystick that operated the ailerons. Push forward and it would make the glider dive, pull back to climb, and move left or right to start banking into a turn. I didn't realise at the time quite how much Guy's introduction to these basic aircraft controls would help me to understand their workings when we started looking at the science of flight.

Right: If I looked like I was a bit nervous about taking control of Guy Westgate's glider, it's because I was!

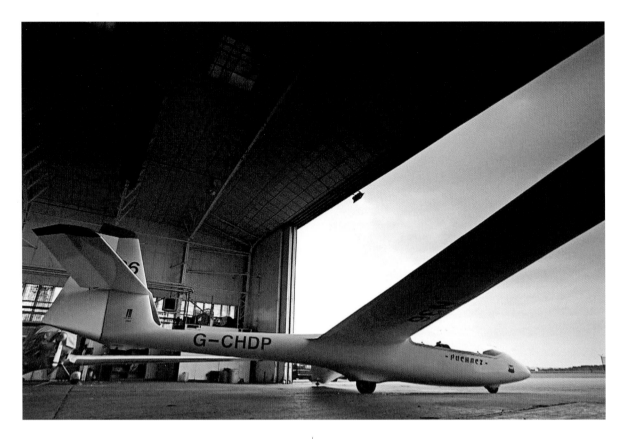

Above: The Puchacz glider, a Polish design, had one main undercarriage wheel just behind the cockpit and a smaller one below the nose.

Strapped into the seat with the Perspex bubble canopy closed, it felt quite roomy inside but, like a rally car or Dave Jenkins's racing truck, there were no creature comforts – just an air vent in the instrument panel. It makes sense. Why would you want to install any kind of fancy trim when what you really need to do is to save weight wherever you can?

Gliders generally take off and land using just one wheel below the cockpit area and a tail skid. When the tow plane started dragging us forward, the wings were levelled out and we were rumbling off down the runway, but not for long. We were in the air in no time, flying smoothly behind the tow plane up to around 4,000 feet (just over 1,200 metres), at which point the tow cable was released and we were on our own.

Guy showed me some basic manoeuvres, banking left and right, explaining how to use the rudder pedals along with the control stick, and then he let me have a go. I knew he was right behind me and could take over if I made a hash of it, but I still felt a bit nervous handling a glider on my very first flight! The controls were incredibly sensitive and needed a very gentle touch, but I managed to change direction without sending us hurtling towards the ground. That would come next.

Guy wanted to demonstrate how a wing will stall. He pulled the nose up and our air speed started to drop off. Suddenly the whole glider pitched forward, there was a huge noise of wind rush and from the front seat I had an excellent view of the ground rushing towards us! As calm and smooth as you like, Guy pulled us out of the dive, and peace and quiet returned to the cockpit. That was a hair-raising, rollercoaster stunt that had made me feel I was going to throw up – not the sort of thing you want to repeat in a hurry, except that I did. Of course I wanted to do it again. Diving towards the ground like that was a fantastic feeling – raw speed and a real element of danger – but ultimately you are in control and if you do everything right you come out of it unscathed. It doesn't get much better than that, does it? Then Guy told me it was my turn to try a stall, and I almost changed my mind. You can't back down from a challenge, though, can you? So I took the controls and pulled the nose up. Actually, I pulled the nose up a bit sharpish and we stalled even more spectacularly, dropping into the dive far more suddenly than I expected, but I followed Guy's instructions and we gently pulled out.

From the moment a glider is release by its tow plane, it starts to lose height, unless the pilot can use an area of warm rising air, a thermal, to soar upwards. Generally, once you are down to around 800 feet (250 metres) it's time to land. Guy, however, is one of only a handful of glider pilots skilled enough to be allowed to 'buzz' the runway at a height of only five feet (1.5 metres) and a speed of up to 130 mph. I couldn't stop grinning. I had never been that fast, that close to the ground, without an engine, and walked away with no broken bones!

Having picked up so much speed diving towards the runway, Guy was able to climb away from the runway in a banking turn and then bring us in for a proper landing.

Back on the ground, he was actually very complimentary about my flying, telling the rest of our crew that I had 'fantastic hand-eye co-ordination' and that I had 'picked up everything really quickly, demonstrating that he could keep the aircraft under control'. I was chuffed with Guy's assessment, but flying the glider had raised a few concerns about taking control of an HPA. In the glider I was able to control it using my hands and feet while sitting comfortably strapped into a seat. I was able to see all around me, keep my eye on the horizon and even look at the instruments to check that I was flying straight and level while we were sailing around the sky.

From what I had seen of HPAs up to that point, my feet would be on bicycle pedals, not rudder pedals, and checking the horizon and operating aircraft controls wasn't going to be easy while pedalling like billy-o. I guess that's why more people have been to the moon than have flown HPAs.

Above: The glider's controls were quite sensitive, but once I started to get the hang of things I was having a ball!

Following page: The view from the cockpit was out of this world.

Understanding Wings and Things

The Science of Flying and Gliding

In order to break the record I needed to talk to someone who could help me to understand all of the challenges we would face in trying to fly an HPA.

DR ALEX Forrester who works down at Southampton University was just the man for the job. Alex is a hugely qualified aerospace engineer and design engineer whose ideas have been used in creating gas turbines, sports equipment, satellites and Formula One racing cars. Most important of all, he was leading a team of students at the university who intended to design and build their own HPA.

Southampton has long been associated with the aircraft industry, the Supermarine Aviation Works having been established in the town about 100 years ago. They built the Spitfire, a highly advanced aeroplane in its day and one of the most beautiful aircraft ever to take to the skies, its designer Reginald Mitchell creating a real masterpiece. Supermarine no longer exists as an aircraft manufacturer, but Southampton is still at the cutting edge of aircraft design and research and the students at Southampton University are all well aware of the famous SUMPAC success. Following in the SUMPAC's footsteps is a pretty tall order, but Alex Forrester and his team reckoned they had a few new ideas to bring to the party. His first job, though, was to explain to me a few basic principles of flight – how an aircraft gets off the ground and what keeps it in the air.

When it comes to the forces that are involved in getting an aircraft to fly, there are four major players in the game – thrust, drag, lift and weight.

Thrust in a normal aeroplane comes from the propeller or the jet engine. The Spitfire had its propeller in the nose, and the spinning prop pulled the fighter through the air. A Jumbo Jet has four jet engines that blow gas out behind them to push the airliner along.

Drag is something I already knew quite a bit about, not least from the way we had to deal with it during the 'Britain's Fastest Bike' challenge. When an object is moving through a liquid – and, if you think back to the previous chapter, we can consider air as acting just like a liquid – the friction that is created acts against thrust, pushing against the object. If we have more drag than thrust, our aircraft will slow down; but if we have more thrust than drag, it will go faster.

Lift is something that is created when a wing or foil moves through a liquid. The shape of the wing pushing the liquid aside is what creates lift. If you were to slice through a wing to look at its cross-section, you would see a kind of elongated teardrop shape. Although

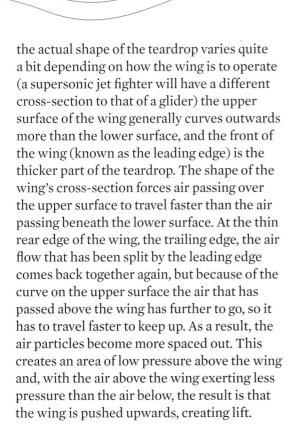

the actual shape of the teardrop varies quite a bit depending on how the wing is to operate (a supersonic jet fighter will have a different cross-section to that of a glider) the upper surface of the wing generally curves outwards more than the lower surface, and the front of the wing (known as the leading edge) is the thicker part of the teardrop. The shape of the wing's cross-section forces air passing over the upper surface to travel faster than the air passing beneath the lower surface. At the thin rear edge of the wing, the trailing edge, the air flow that has been split by the leading edge comes back together again, but because of the curve on the upper surface the air that has passed above the wing has further to go, so it has to travel faster to keep up. As a result, the air particles become more spaced out. This creates an area of low pressure above the wing and, with the air above the wing exerting less pressure than the air below, the result is that the wing is pushed upwards, creating lift.

Everything on Earth has weight (some people have more than others!), which is a combination of mass and the effect of gravity. It is easy to confuse mass and weight, and for the purposes of working out how an aeroplane flies we have to think of weight as a downward force in order to balance it with the other forces (thrust, drag and lift) that are at work.

This is where Sir Isaac Newton crops up again. According to Newton's 'Second Law of Motion' (the one we skipped over in the first chapter) force (F) is a product of mass (m) and acceleration (a). Force is measured in Newtons, named after good old Sir Isaac, mass is measured in kilograms, and the acceleration involved is the effect of gravity. Gravity is the thing that attracts everything in the universe towards everything else. That means that you are attracting the earth towards you but, because the earth is so much bigger than you and has so much more mass, its gravitational pull is far greater than yours. If you jump in the air, the earth pulls you back towards it, rather than the earth being pulled towards you. The effect of the earth's gravitational pull causes objects to accelerate towards it at 9.8 metres per second per second. The figure of 9.8 metres per second is about 22 mph, meaning that an object falling towards the earth will accelerate from rest to 22 mph after the first second, 44 mph after the next second and so on. The scientists and engineers use metres per second rather than miles per hour in their calculations, which is why the acceleration is given as 9.8 metres per second (the speed) per second (the rate of acceleration). To avoid writing 9.8 metres per second per second all the time, it is normally written as 9.8 metres per second squared – 9.8m/s^2.

Lift is the force generated by the way that the forward movement created by the thrust causes air to rush over the wings. The air particles passing over the upper, curved surface of the wing have further to go than those passing over the flat underside of the wing. This means that the particles above the wing are spaced further out, creating lower air pressure above the wing than below, pushing the wing upwards.

Drag

Drag is air resistance, even more of a problem when trying to fly than it was when I was trying to break the cycle speed record. Every part of the aircraft that is exposed to the air suffers from friction with the air particles pushing against them or passing over them, causing drag to work against thrust.

Lift

Lift

Lift

Strangely, thrust for our HPA would be created in part by friction, which is also a major element of drag, against which thrust is fighting. The friction helping to create thrust in this case is what gives the rubber tyres their traction with the runway. Without that grip, I would not be able to make any headway and there would be no thrust.

Thrust

Weight

Weight is obviously what something weighs, right? Actually, when you think of weight as a force, it's a bit more complicated than that. Weight is the effect that gravity has on the mass of any given thing. That's why an astronaut on the Moon, who has the same mass that he did when he was on Earth, has a different weight. Fortunately, we wouldn't be going as far as the Moon.

This simple calculation would help Alex and his team to work out how much thrust would need to come from pedal power to overcome the drag and the weight in order for the wing to be moving through the air fast enough to generate the lift required to get the HPA airborne.

Weight is a force (F) created by gravity. Gravity supplies the acceleration (a) and your mass (m) is you. In outer space, where there is zero gravity, you would still have your mass (all your bits would still be present), but your weight (the force F) would be zero. In space you are weightless.

Accele

So, if an object has a mass (m) of 10 kg, to find its weight as a force (F) we multiply 10 by the acceleration caused by gravity, 9.8m/s², and come up with a force of 98 Newtons.

F = m x a

eration

Pedal Power

Getting up to Speed

We may have been at Calshot to cycle, but we were starting our HPA speed campaign at the historic heart of air racing!

CALSHOT Velodrome is just a short journey from Southampton and is the only indoor banked velodrome cycle track in the South of England. The velodrome is part of Calshot Activities Centre, a huge adventure centre on a spit of land that sticks out into the Solent. Here you can learn and take part in all sorts of watersports, while inside the giant aircraft hangar it also offers skiing on a dry ski slope, rock climbing and cycle racing. The hangar was the base for the Sunderland flying boats and at one time housed the RAF's High Speed Flight, the lads who competed in the Schneider Trophy races. Having taken the trophy in 1927 and 1929 (the race was held every two years) against stiff international competition, in 1931 the High Speed Flight won the competition for the third time in a row, meaning that the trophy was theirs to keep forever. The seaplane they raced was the Supermarine S.6B, a direct ancestor of the Spitfire.

The velodrome can be a busy place, as it is used not only by individual cyclists taking the racing courses laid on at the velodrome but also by cycling clubs and even Olympic cyclists as a training venue – but we were lucky enough to have it to ourselves for a while. As I changed into cycling togs, Alex explained what we were about to do. He had a very nice Cannondale racer for me to ride, and it had been fitted with strain gauges that would give me an electronic read-out on a handlebar display showing how much power I was delivering. Alex also had a screen that would show him how I was doing. I was to do circuits of 133 metres and go for 15 laps in three minutes. Alex and his team had calculated how much drag their design would incur and that it would have a mass of 110 kilograms with me on board. The power output reading that I would see on my display was in watts and I needed to aim for 450 watts. To give you an idea of how much effort that requires, it has been estimated that a man doing manual labour can keep up an average output over an eight-hour day of 75 watts. Sprinter Usain Bolt was measured at one point during a record-breaking 100 metres race generating more than 2,600 watts, although his average over the race (he can do 100 metres in 9.58 seconds) was closer to 1,500 watts. That is about the same as a Tour de France cyclist during a finishing sprint, although they will probably generate about 500 watts during most of the rest of the stage. I reckoned that keeping to a steady 450 watts over three minutes would not be a problem. How wrong I was.

Once I got going on the first lap, the read-out was easily topping 500 watts. On the second lap I was settling in to around the 450-watt target area, and then the figures started to slide. Nobody could ever accuse me of being a slacker, or of being unfit, but, even with all of the training that I had been putting in for the 'Britain's Fastest Bike' challenge, my lungs simply could not feed my muscles fast enough. My legs felt OK, but I was puffing like an old steam engine and after five laps the power output was all over the place. When Alex flagged me down after 15 laps, I could barely speak, I was gasping for breath so much. Clearly I had some work to do, but figuring out how best to improve my performance threw up a few surprises – including beetroot.

The reason that I was aiming for a target of three minutes producing 450 watts was, obviously, that 450 watts was what Alex and his boffins reckoned I needed to produce to get the HPA off the ground. The three-minute element was the time that an average HPA flight lasts and, if I was going for speed, it would be all that I would need. If I could crank out the required 450 watts, it would, in theory, take me to around 28 mph on the ground and, once in the air, we might make 30 mph or more. The big difference between this challenge and the 'Fastest Bike' challenge was that riding behind Dave Jenkins's truck I was towed up to the operating speed and my legs, with my feet locked to the pedals, were turning all the way. When the tow cable was released, I had to keep my legs turning and increase the effort, which was tough, but I wasn't starting entirely from scratch. With the HPA I would have to

power it from a standing start to 28 mph and I needed to do that as quickly as possible. Alex's calculations indicated that I would need to be cranking out 600 watts to achieve take-off before settling down to the 450-watt output that would maintain level flight. This meant that I needed two different kinds of power delivery – explosive power to get me going and then sustained power to keep me airborne.

It is not easy to get that variety of power delivery from the same muscle groups. Think of it in terms of cars. The fastest drag racers are built purely for acceleration and can reach

Fast Twitch

or

Slow Twitch

100 mph from a standing start in less than 1 second, but they are designed purely to shoot down a quarter-mile of drag strip tarmac. If you wanted to cruise down a motorway at 100 mph (where that's legal!) for any length of time, you would choose an Aston Martin or a Bentley – completely different animals from the drag racer. You have the same sort of thing going on with muscles in your body.

All of your muscles are made up of what are known as slow-twitch and fast-twitch fibres. Most of your muscles have a mixture of both, but the big muscles like the soleus muscle in your lower leg and the muscles in your back that you use all the time simply to keep you standing upright contain mainly slow-twitch fibres. The muscles in your eyes that help you give something a quick sideways glance are mostly fast-twitch fibres. The different kinds of fibres produce power in different ways. Slow-twitch fibres need lots of oxygen to do their job, which means they need a strong blood supply, the oxygen in the blood providing the energy to make the muscles contract. The slow-twitch muscles deliver steady power over a long period. Fast-twitch muscle fibres don't need so much oxygen because they produce a small burst of energy, their muscle contraction being over and done with in the blink of an eye. In fact, that's exactly what the blink of an eye is – a fast-twitch muscle in action.

Your eyes, which you can move and blink incredibly quickly, use fast-twitch muscle fibres for blinking or making a quick sideways glance, whereas your legs use slow-twitch muscle fibres for standing and walking. You can teach the muscles in your legs to act more like fast-twitch fibres, and that's what athletes like Usain Bolt have to do to produce the explosive power delivery that made him the fastest human on the planet. Obviously years of training are required for that and there are some things that scientists have proved help with the training – such as the humble beetroot.

Beetroot juice is packed full of nitrates which your body converts into nitric oxide, and this has the effect of widening the blood vessels to increase blood flow while also reducing the amount of oxygen that the muscles need to do their job. Lots of top sports people swear by beetroot juice, so it had to be worth giving it a try, but beetroot superfuel alone wasn't going to get me to 450 watts for three minutes, so I fitted a strain gauge to my own bike and got down to some serious training.

Making sure that the human engine could do its job was one part of the challenge, but the most important part was the HPA itself, so it was back to Southampton University to take a look at the design and lend a hand in building the aircraft that I was to fly.

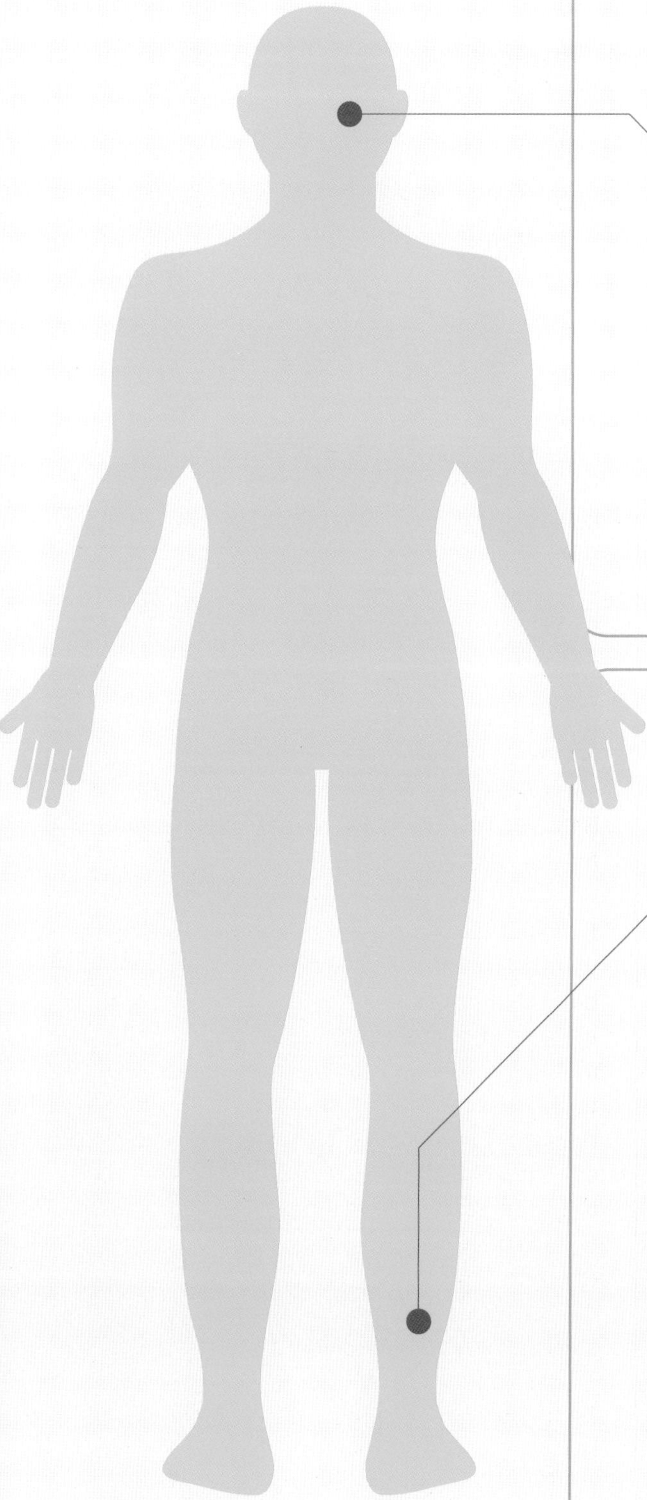

Fast Twitch

Eye muscle

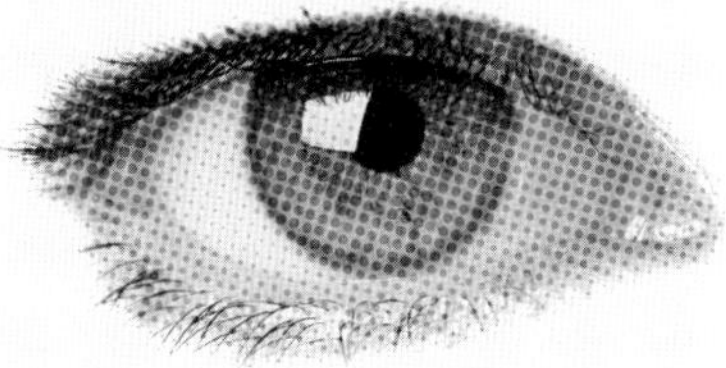

Anaerobic

Produces a **small** amount of energy,

fast

Slow Twitch

Soleus

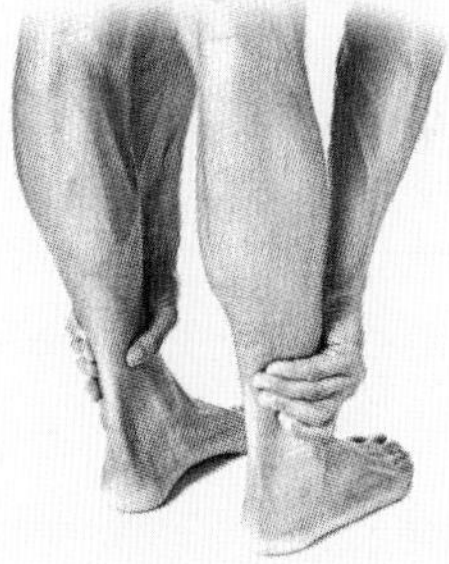

(it's the lower calf muscle)

Aerobic

Produces a **large** amount of energy,

s l o w l y

Building a Record Breaker

The SUHPA (Southampton University Human Powered Aircraft) team had come up with a design that looked simple and elegant, although that doesn't do justice to the ingenuity that went into creating it.

THE whole thing was based around a carbon-fibre racing bike that was completely enclosed inside a cockpit capsule coated with transparent film. The cockpit was a framework of lightweight foam – a bit like the kind of rigid foam that is used in packaging to protect electrical goods – that then had a sort of clingfilm stretched over it to seal the pilot inside a streamlined hull.

Above the pilot's fairing was a wing 20 metres (66 feet) across made from sections of rigid foam, and a black tail boom that reached back to a tail section that had the horizontal and vertical surfaces you would expect to see on a normal aircraft except that these too were made of rigid foam covered with transparent film.

Rotating around the tail boom just behind the cockpit was a large propeller with two blades, each about 1.5 metres (5 feet) long. Driven by a chain system from the rear wheel of the bike,

Top: The bicycle chains showing the gears for driving the bike forwards and the big gear with the chain running up to the propeller shaft.

Bottom: To avoid using an energy-sapping gear system, the prop-shaft chain was guided round in a 'twist' to turn the cog on the shaft.

the propeller blades were also made mainly from rigid foam.

The frame that attached the tail boom to the bike, the boom itself and the main spar inside the foam wing were all made from carbon-fibre reinforced polymer, an incredibly strong but amazingly light material. Saving weight, of course, was essential and the whole aircraft, with its massive wingspan, was designed to weigh just 33 kilograms – that's only about the weight of an average Labrador dog!

Alex explained that pedalling the bike along a runway would be what got me into the air. If I could get to over 25 mph on the ground, that would create enough air flow over the wing to generate the lift we needed. Once the wheels were off the ground, their job was done and the propeller would take over. The gearing on the bike was such that, by the time I reached take-off speed, the propeller would be operating at its optimum efficiency and would provide all the thrust we needed.

With the wheels off the ground, I would no longer have what little control I'd had when steering the aircraft by using the bike. From now on I would be steering the HPA the way a pilot does.

As I learned from Guy Westgate, making any aircraft go where you want it to is basically a case of changing the shape of the wing. We've seen how air flow over the wing generates lift, as lower pressure is created above the wing

Top: The SUHPA's only movable control surfaces were in the tail, powered by remotely controlled electric motors.

Bottom: The chain linking to the prop-shaft cog, nestling between the wings.

by its shape forcing the air to move faster. If you change the shape of the wing, obviously you alter the air flow and that can help you to generate either more or less lift. In the wings and tails of most aeroplanes there are movable flaps which are known as control surfaces.

I'm more a spanners and hammers man – but it was obviously going to be fun helping put the HPA together.

The control surfaces in the wings are called ailerons. These work as opposites, so that if the pilot pushes his joystick or control column left, then the left wing aileron flap is raised and the right one lowered. This changes the air flow over the wings so that the left wing generates less lift than the right wing. As a result the right wing rises, causing the aircraft to bank left. There are similar control surfaces in the tail. On the horizontal tail 'wing' there are flaps called elevators. These work together to raise or lower the tail, thereby pointing the nose of the aeroplane upwards or downwards. In the upright 'fin' of the tail there is a rudder which works just like the rudder on a ship, helping to point the nose of the plane either right or left.

Our HPA was going to do without control surfaces in the wings, but the tail was to have both rudder and elevators. Steering the HPA with the rudder would give us all the control we needed. A dynamic, banking turn when you are just a few feet off the ground and your wingspan is more than 60 feet is almost bound to end in you ploughing a furrow with your wingtip and bringing the whole HPA crashing to the ground. Best to avoid that, really. I would find out later exactly how to operate these controls. In the meantime, we had an aeroplane to build, and this was going to involve messing about with foam.

Lightweight foam and clingfilm aren't really the sort of materials I'm used to working with – I'm more a spanners and hammers man – but it was obviously going to be fun helping put the HPA together, and the whole process had to start with the manufacture of the parts.

Constructing the Wings

Messing about in foam might make you think of one of those parties, but the foam we were about to mess about with was far more serious stuff. Ben Tindale was my guide to working with foam. An expert in robotics engineering, Australian-born Ben has built some fantastic machines for his company, Tindale Systems, to manufacture all manner of tools and components. He was to take the CAD (computer aided design) blueprints from Alex's team and turn them into actual components. The machines Ben worked with produced components that were accurately engineered to within fractions of a millimetre, yet he too, like Alex and his team, applied a 'suck it and see', trial-and-error approach to the HPA. Despite all the time they spent on painstaking calculations, they were always willing to go back to the drawing board if something didn't work. Ben described projects like the HPA as encompassing his 'Holy Trinity', as he put it: 'You think a bit; you build a bit; then you go out and hurt yourself. It's amazing how you can come up with a better idea when your knees are bleeding!'

A bit of a joker he may be, but Ben's machines were something else. With the CAD design for a wing section programmed into his foam fabrication machine, I stood back and marvelled

Above: The left wing tip and aileron flap.

Above: The root of the wing showing the structure of the foam ribs and the main alloy spar.

Above: A brew always helps when you're trying to work out maths or science, and the big mug of tea came in very handy.

Previous page: SUHPA was easily light enough to carry, but we had to take care with it because it was also light enough to blow away!

Right: The propeller was fastened to a large diameter pipe with the tail boom running inside it.

at the way it went about its job. A solid block of foam was clamped in place and then a stretched wire, which Ben described as 'like the E string on a guitar', was guided into position by the machine. The wire had an electric current passing through it that made it heat up, and it then passed through the foam like a knife through butter. Using the hot wire, smooth curves and tight angles could be cut that would be impossible to do using any kind of blade.

> We had some work to do there, but Alex's SUHPA team weren't slow to roll up their sleeves and get the job done.

The wire was able to cut shaped sections of wing that had a smooth, curved outer surface (the top surface of the wing) and bracing ribs in the inner surface that would maintain the shape of the wing. The wire also cut a separate lower wing surface, and the idea was that these would then be glued together to make a wing segment. On previous HPAs, wings had been made using balsa wood or foam ribs over which they stretched plastic film that was then heated with a hot-air gun (the sort of thing you might use for stripping paint) to form a tight skin. This was a tried and tested technique – it was the way that we were going to build our cockpit – but stretching the film across ribs over the entire length of the wing tended to give a 'scalloped', uneven surface to the upper wing, disturbing the air flow. The SUHPA's wing would be smooth – to help maximise speed. By the time we had glued the two sections together and smoothed it all down by hand for a perfect finish, we had spent almost half a day on one wing section – and it would take 32 of these to

make up each wing. We had some work to do there, but Alex's SUHPA team weren't slow to roll up their sleeves and get the job done.

Carving the Propeller

Another of Ben's machines was used to make the propeller blades, also manufactured from foam. This was a computer-controlled milling machine that went to work on a solid block of foam and simply shredded the bits it didn't want, carving a perfect propeller shape from the block like a robot sculptor. Turn the block over and it carved out the other side of the blade. In fact, it could cut three blades from one big block of foam – only the best ones would be used on the HPA.

Once the blades were cut, they were covered with a thin sheet of glass-fibre fabric that was painted with an epoxy resin that bonds the fabric to the foam, strengthening and stiffening the whole structure while still allowing it to flex. On its own, the foam would be too fragile to handle the stress that a propeller blade has to cope with. The resin was left to dry overnight and then the blades had to be sanded down very carefully to produce a perfectly smooth surface. A propeller blade really is a thing of beauty. Essentially, it does the same job as a wing and is shaped like a slightly twisted wing. As the propeller blade spins, air moves across its surface creating the same sort of pressure differences that give a wing its lift, only in the case of the propeller the difference in pressure is generating thrust. To make sure that our propeller was going to be up to the job, we took it to Southampton University's R.J. Mitchell wind tunnel, named after the man who designed the Supermarine Spitfire.

The Mitchell wind tunnel has been used for a wide variety of aerodynamic testing, including

Above: The SUHPA had to be assembled on site at Sywell Aerodrome and from this angle you can see the remote control set-up that operated the tailplane control surfaces.

work on Formula One cars. Basically, it's a big fan that blows air through a tunnel so that you can test how well your aerodynamic devices are working. A wing relies on air flow over its surface to generate lift, and that flow can come from it being pushed through the air by an engine, or by the air being pushed against the wing. Sometimes a mixture of both does the trick. When you're flying a kite (which is basically a wing) you might have to run a bit to

In the wind tunnel we set up the bike attached to the HPA frame only – no wings or tail, just the propeller on its tail boom mounting. I did the pedalling to get the propeller spinning at speed and the wind tunnel provided the air flow. We hit a couple of problems, the first one when the chain came off, something that every cyclist has to deal with at some time or other – usually in the dark when it's pouring with rain and you're miles from home. We needed to get the tension on the chain exactly right. Too tight and it might snap, too loose and it would be wasting energy and likely to pop off.

The next setback taught us a proper lesson. I heard an almighty whack from behind me as I was pedalling and then everyone yelling at me to stop. It turned out that the propeller had hit the rear of the cockpit frame. It seems that it was flexing too much at low speed. At higher speed it would be fine, but as we were building up speed it had bent a bit, smacked the back of the frame and one of the blades was broken. Knowing how much effort we had put in to make the blades, I was gutted, but Alex and Ben were quite philosophical about it. For Ben, this was a 'bleeding knees' lesson, and Alex's attitude was simply that it was better for this to happen now than for it to happen when we were out trying to fly our HPA. A crashed HPA can take a lot of repairing, as I knew from the length of time it had taken to make just one wing section.

We decided to use the 'reject' blades to make a stiffer propeller. We needed the quickest solution because time was no longer on our side. We were now working to a deadline, with only a month to get our HPA in flying condition for an event known as the Icarus Cup.

get the air flow, but once it's up in the wind the breeze is supplying the air flow that makes it fly. If you've ever watched a war movie where there's an aircraft carrier involved, you'll know they turn the ship into the wind so that the planes taking off have air flow from the wind passing over their wings as well as thrust from their engines, helping their wings to generate lift by the time they reach the end of the deck – otherwise they would get very wet.

The Ground Breakers

The Icarus Cup is an annual event for HPAs and is organised by the RAeS. I went to get some inspiration from a team who'd been there in the early days.

T HE competition is run over several days and involves different challenges such as the longest flight, a 200-metre sprint, a 1-kilometre race, a slalom course, accuracy in take-off and landing, and a race round a triangular course. 'But why?' I hear you ask. 'Surely all of these things were done by HPA teams years ago?' You're not wrong, but the way they are trying to do them nowadays is very different from the way they were done back in the day.

One of the aims of the RAeS is to encourage the development of HPAs so that human powered flying can become a sport in which enthusiasts can compete against each other – like hang-gliding or sailing. With that aim in mind, they are encouraging people to design their own HPAs, but the new designs have to be an attempt to make the HPA a more practical vehicle. The Kremer Prize winners were brilliant machines, but they were very fragile.

If HPA flying was to become a recreational sport, the RAeS wanted teams to come up with aircraft that could be flown under any reasonable conditions. Not only that, they wanted aircraft kits that could easily be transported to a venue and assembled. Our SUHPA design had a standard racing bike at its heart, and the rest of it could easily be broken down to fit into the back of a large car. It was a fair way from something that anyone

Above: The SUMPAC, clad in its full outer skin, looks reasonably robust, but the slightest damage caused during any of the 35 failed flight attempts meant long hours of repair work.

could bolt together at a moment's notice, but it was certainly in keeping with the spirit of the RAeS's plans for HPAs.

If we were going to fly our HPA in a competition, I wanted to get some flying tips from people who had been through what I was going to have to do – and who better than the SUMPAC (Southampton University Man Powered Aircraft) flyers who made that first historic flight back in 1961. Some never left the protection of their hangars if there was any chance of a wind stronger than 4 mph, and attempting a turn was not something that you did if there was a wind of 1 mph.

At an elegant Victorian house in Barnes, South West London, I met with one of the original SUMPAC designers, Alan Lassiere, and the man who piloted the aircraft, Derek Piggott. In 1960 Alan and two other Southampton University students, Anne Marsden and David Williams, decided to design and build an HPA. They used balsa wood, lightweight aluminium alloy and a kind of nylon to form the skin of the aircraft. The material was painted with silver dope, a kind of varnish that has been used in various forms since the early days of flight to treat fabric when it is used on the fuselage and wings of an aircraft. Dope serves to stiffen the cloth as well as making it wind- and waterproof. The three students, who were studying for their final exams, and the friends they roped in to help them build the SUMPAC had to squeeze their design, build and development time in between studying and lectures.

'We would work all night using our wind tunnel to get the design sorted out,' Alan told me, 'and it was so noisy that the neighbours complained to the university.' SUMPAC took 40,000 man hours to build, using 35,000 individual parts. A crash could set them back weeks, and crash they did.

Derek Piggott became involved when the group took the SUMPAC to Lasham Airfield in Hampshire, where he was the chief gliding instructor. Lasham had been an RAF base during the Second World War but had been home to various gliding clubs since the early 1950s. Derek, who had trained as a pilot with the RAF in 1942 and had gone on to become one of their top flying and gliding instructors, was fascinated by the SUMPAC project, but he wasn't the first-choice pilot.

'We had a top cyclist lined up to fly the thing,' Derek explained, 'but we simply couldn't teach him to fly, so I ended up doing the pedalling.' The SUMPAC team really could not have hoped for a better-qualified pilot. Derek has flown thousands of hours in more than 150 different types of powered aircraft and 180 different types of glider, yet even he found the SUMPAC difficult to handle. The 35 attempts that the team made before Derek finally got the aircraft off the ground often ended in disaster. 'Even something as simple as drifting off the edge of the runway would result in a broken main wheel,' Derek said.

When they eventually did see their aircraft take off – albeit that its first flight only lasted for 8 seconds – Alan remembers the reaction of the team. 'We just stood there,' he said. 'Disbelief.' Both Alan and Derek were clearly very proud to have been part of the team that created the first successful HPA. Their enthusiasm, still fresh after more than half a century, was an inspiration to me. Having met them, I wanted to set a new speed record more than ever. The Germans had held the record for the best part of 30 years – it was time we claimed it for Britain.

Above: Without its skin, the SUMPAC's light but fragile skeleton shows how easy it was to damage the structure.

Natural Born Flyers

However clever our engineers become, they will always struggle to match the variety of flying techniques that birds have developed through millions of years of evolution.

QUITE naturally, a bird wants to be able to cover as much ground as it needs to while wasting as little energy as possible. Birds flap their wings, using fast-twitch muscle fibres to push them forwards to generate lift but that requires a lot of energy. Once they are in the air, birds can 'soar' to great heights on rising currents of air, the height then allowing them to glide long distances without having to flap too hard. Birds of prey such as kestrels can hover, turning into the wind and flapping their wings to hold themselves stationary in the air while they scan the ground for a tasty mouse or other scurrying creature. Then, they swoop.

To follow fast-moving prey on the ground, a bird of prey might swoop very low, gliding along at daffodil height with barely a twitch of its wing. When they are doing this they are demonstrating how well they have mastered a phenomenon known as 'ground effect'. We have seen how the airflow over a wing creates a difference in pressure that generates lift but where the surface of the wing comes to an end at the wing tip, a disturbance is created that causes a swirling vortex of air. This normally acts as an extra form of drag, reducing the lift generated by the wing, but when the wing is close to the ground, the vortex can't form properly and without its drag factor the wing generates lift more efficiently.

The close proximity of the ground also compresses the air between the bird and the ground, increasing the pressure beneath the wing even more than in normal flight and again producing more lift. Flying low, then, is a good way of covering ground using the least amount of energy. Can this really work for aircraft as well as birds? In the late 1980s, the Soviet navy had a seaplane called a Lun Ekranoplan which was one of the biggest aeroplanes ever built, longer than a 747 jumbo jet and powered by eight jet engines. It was designed as a missile platform and cruised at a height of less than 4 metres (13 feet), using the ground effect 'air cushion' created by its wings to keep it flying just above the waves.

Below: The different stages involved in one flap of a bird's wings, showing how lift is generated.

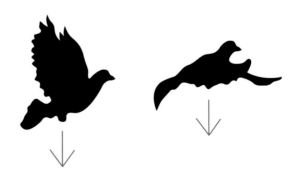

Ground effect would be of little use to me because I wouldn't have the speed to enjoy its benefits and I wasn't going to be able to vary the way I flapped my wings, so I would just have to rely on good old pedal power!

In order to achieve thrust and lift, I was going to have to pedal like the clappers, but birds do it simply by flapping their wings. Yet the wing flap is not as simple as it looks. A bird's wing generates lift in exactly the same way as an aircraft wing, using the difference in pressure created by air flowing over and under the wing. Small birds jump or hop forwards to generate the initial airflow while larger birds run into the wind.

Once airborne, a bird's wings also turn into its propellers when the bird flaps. Different areas of the wing have different jobs to do. The part closest to the body moves least and provides basic lift, but when the bird flaps its wings downwards it is also pushing part of the wing forwards, tilted at an angle. This changes the airflow over that part of the wing so that the 'lift' is in a forward direction rather than straight up. This is actually what our propeller is doing when I described it earlier as being like 'a slightly twisted wing'. The feathers on the wing, meanwhile, are performing all sorts of other important tasks.

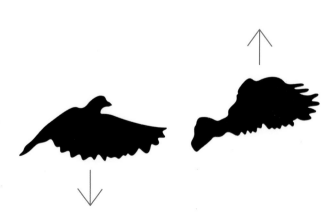

A bird's wing has evolved over millions of years. There is a large muscle mass close to the body that supplies the power strokes for flapping, smaller muscles along the wing that control the primary flight feathers at the wingtips, and the secondary flight feathers at the rear or 'trailing edge' of the wing.

Primary flight feathers
The feathers at the wing tip and outer edge of the wing provide the majority of the thrust. They can also be separated and rotated so that they don't cause negative thrust when the wing is in the upward stroke of a flap.

Secondary flight feathers

The secondaries give the wing its 'foil' shape to provide lift. Along with the retrices – tail feathers – these help the bird to steer and control its speed.

Slots

The slots are created when the primaries are separated. These can be used to channel air from below the wing. Vortices of turbulent air that contribute to drag can be controlled and used to provide extra lift when the bird feeds that air through the slots.

Covert feathers

These feathers grow in rows lying on top of each other like roof tiles to help streamline the bird, improving airflow over the wing.

Taking Control
Testing and Modifying

I'd been putting in the training hours and was pretty confident that I would be able to supply the required levels of power, but controlling the HPA on take-off would be crucial.

THE latest calculations factoring in the new propeller showed that the prop reached its optimum efficiency at 28 mph – any slower than that and it would feel like I was pedalling through treacle. That meant I would have to be pedalling along the ground pretty much at the record speed just to make sure that I could achieve take-off.

The flaps in the tail would have to be raised to bring the nose up. This would change the 'angle of attack' of the wing – the angle at which it cuts into the air flow – and generate that rush of lift that I needed to get off the ground. Once airborne, the HPA would suddenly become vulnerable to any slight crosswind, having lost the grip on the tarmac that helped me to keep it heading in a straight line. I would have to use the rudder to stay on course.

Rather than having a complicated arrangement of control cables, Alex and his team had come up with a clever solution. The rudder and elevators would work just like those in a model aeroplane using an RC (remote control) handset. The plan was to attach the handset to the handlebars, where I would have it within easy reach.

Left: I concentrate hard on keeping the model glider 'flying' straight and level in a wind-tunnel-style flow of air.

Top: Using the remote to adjust the control surfaces required both hands, which would be a problem for me while I was pedalling the SUHPA.

Bottom: We used a stream of smoke to study how air flowed over the surface of the wing.

Following page: Ribbons on a stick were also useful to show smooth air flow and turbulence.

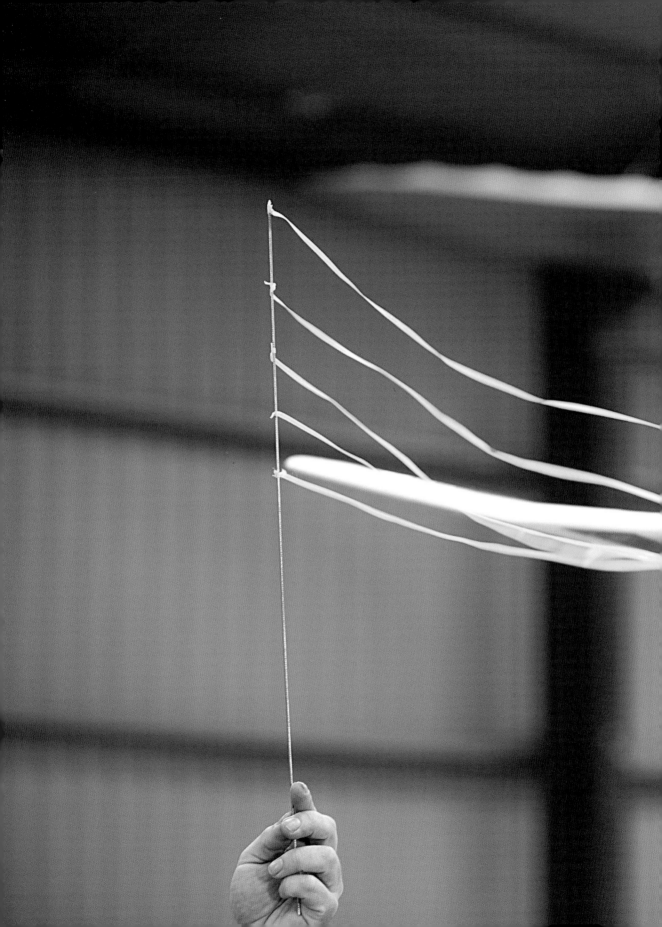

The Moment of Truth

At four o'clock in the morning one day in mid July I was standing in the fresh air enjoying a brew outside a hangar at Lasham Airfield, waiting for the lads inside to finish putting the SUHPA together.

WE HAD arrived the previous evening and had started assembling our aircraft, but I had been sent off to get some kip while the rest of the team soldiered on. I'll never say a word ever again about students being lazy beggars, especially the ones at Southampton. SUMPAC students had worked through the night on their aircraft and here we were, more than fifty years later, with another bunch of Southampton students putting in some proper graft. Three of them, Jacob, Ruben and Chris, had carried on working with Alex and Ben while I got my head down to make sure that I could pummel those pedals.

Also on hand was a very experienced HPA expert, Dr Bill Brooks. Chairman of the RAeS human-powered flight group and a highly qualified aircraft designer, Bill is the man who runs the Icarus Cup. He had been there in the background all along, advising us on our HPA build, and now that we were about to give it a whirl for the first time he was to play a very active part in the proceedings. While I pedalled the HPA down the runway, he would be keeping pace with the aircraft on another bike, operating the remote control handset. With the responsibility of the rudder and elevators out of my hands – quite literally – all I had to concentrate on was generating the power to get us airborne.

Above: Once I was sealed into the cockpit there wasn't much elbow room, but keeping the SUHPA light meant no wasted space.

Despite all the work that had been put in, the sectional foam wing wasn't quite ready. We still had a couple of weeks before the Icarus Cup event, so we were confident that we would have the new wing on the day, and in the meantime we had borrowed a film-covered wing from an earlier HPA model. It wouldn't work as well as we hoped our wing would, but it would let us test out the rest of our HPA set-up.

As the sun's rays were starting to light up the sky, the HPA was rolled out, ready to go. We were making our flying attempt at the crack of dawn because we knew we could rely on still air at this time of day, before the sun had had a chance to heat up the ground, heat up the air and produce movement in the air. I squeezed into the cockpit and was sealed in

– any loose surfaces were taped down to stop them flapping about and creating drag. With the SUHPA lined up for its first run and team members supporting the wings, I cranked the pedals as hard and fast as I could. With my eyes fixed on the horizon to keep me aware of the aircraft's positioning, I pounded the pedals for all I was worth. Then the front wheel rose off the ground and I thought we were about to take to the air, but the rear wheel stayed stubbornly on the ground.

I reckoned I needed to be in a higher gear, so we sorted that out for the next run and the HPA managed a couple of hopeful hops. It must have looked like bouncing more than flying, but we were definitely getting there. The trouble was that the wind was now getting up and our window of opportunity for test flying was fast closing down. I had to dig in hard, give it a bit more and see what we could do on the last attempt.

There was no holding back this time. I went all out for maximum effort and suddenly the nose was up, the tail was levelling out and I was flying! The pedals felt very different with the wheels off the ground but I knew I had to keep that prop turning, keep on pedalling. It didn't last long and I hit the ground pretty hard. The prop was smashed, so that really did mean the end of our test flights for the day, but our HPA had been airborne. It was a short flight, a little over 16 feet (about 5 metres) at a height of around 2 feet (0.6 metres) but I was happy that, first time out, we had got off the runway and that I had experienced the feeling of transition between driving the wheels and driving the propeller. There was lots of whooping and cheering and I had a grin on my face as wide as Lincolnshire. Now I wanted to give it a go with our new wing design – bring on the Icarus Cup!

Top: Carrying the tailplane out to be attached was an awkward job because it had a mind of its own in even the slightest breeze.

Following page: Pre-flight checks out on the runway.

Bottom: I lent a hand wherever I could to assemble the SUHPA, but everyone was keen for me to save my energy for pedalling.

Going for the Record

At the end of July the team assembled at Sywell Aerodrome in Northamptonshire for the Icarus Cup competition.

SYWELL is one of the few airfields that I have been to that actually isn't a former RAF base. From the time it was established 85 years ago, it has been a civilian aerodrome, although it was pressed into service as a training facility and aircraft repair centre during the Second World War. It is now an aviation museum and home to a number of different flying clubs.

There were a handful of other teams who had brought along their aircraft. Some of these were new; others had flown previously but now had experimental new design features. Over the course of a few days they would compete in a number of different disciplines, or tasks: to achieve the longest flight or the shortest take-off; to be fastest over 1 kilometre, 200 metres, a slalom course and a triangular

Top: Until air is passing over the wing to create lift, the lightweight foam structures tend to sag, which could cause damage, so they need a bit of support from the team members.

Middle: The gears, where muscle power would be converted to lift.

Bottom: The cockpit used transparent film stretched over foam ribs to give a streamlined form.

Far right: Where necessary, the transparent film was sealed in place using tape to make sure it wouldn't flap open, letting air rush in and unbalancing the aircraft.

275 mph

Set by Holger
Rochelt in 1985
in the Musculair II

course. Depending on how they did, they would be awarded points, and the team with the most points at the end of the contest would take home the Icarus Cup.

We were under no illusions that we could win the cup. Our whole intention had been to build an HPA that would be fast. Our aim was to get off the ground and hit a record speed. Not all of the other teams competed in all of the events, either. Like us, they were here to do their best, not to pulverise the opposition, and we all wanted to see as many of the HPAs as possible getting airborne. There was a lot of interest in our wing design, which wasn't surprising as

all of the others were using what looked like variations of the film-covered wing. Everyone seemed impressed with the way it was put together, so that was encouraging. Shame, then, that the night before our speed run one of the guys managed to put his head through a wing panel!

On the morning of the speed run I attended a briefing in the canteen where we were told that we could expect light winds of up to 6 mph, but that those would build during the course of the day. To take advantage of the relatively still air in the early morning, the teams all had allotted times for their flight attempts. Once the morning slots were finished, we would be able to try again at dusk when, hopefully, the calmer conditions enjoyed at dawn would return. With the wing panel repaired we were soon lined up for our first flying attempt, but try as

Facing a 10 mph breeze, enough to scupper most other HPAs, we knew that this couldn't count as an official record because the wind over the wing would be working to our advantage, giving us extra lift, although it would also be causing extra drag at low speed, which was something I would have to fight extra hard to overcome. I wanted to concentrate on providing the power, so we went for the same arrangement that we had at Lasham, with Bill Brooks taking charge of the RC unit. Icarus Cup rules stated that the pilot had to be in control of the aircraft, but we were now doing this for the team, not for the cup.

With two of the guys supporting the wings, I stood on the pedals and powered the wheels forward. There was no holding back now – it was all or nothing. I held it straight along the runway and was pumping my legs so hard that I could hear my heart pounding. Then, suddenly, I was off the ground. It was a fantastic feeling, floating through the air, but I kept up the pace on the pedals and SUHPA flew on human power. I stayed in the air for 50 metres (165 feet) at a height of about 3 metres (10 feet) and a speed of 29 mph (over 46 km/h). We'd reached our target but it wasn't a massive record breaker. In any case the speed, although technically faster than the Germans, wouldn't count because of the wind, the short distance covered and having Bill on the RC – but the guys in the team were all jumping about cheering and clapping, and I was as happy as a dog with two tails.

I might I could not get the HPA off the ground. We weren't the only ones having problems. The Betterfly team's HPA didn't take to the air at all that day – though their pilot, David Barford, had already amassed enough points to win the Icarus Cup. Team Airglow, whose HPA was shared by two pilots who came second and third in the contest overall, veered out of control in a gust of wind and crashed into a parked aeroplane. No one was hurt, but it made us all very aware of how a light breeze can affect a 30-kilogram aircraft.

That evening the breeze was still causing the teams problems, so we had the runway all to ourselves. I was determined that we should have something to show for all the effort that our team had put in to get us to Sywell, so we agreed to have one last attempt at a flight.

I had now joined a very select group – people who have pedalled an aeroplane into the air. More people have made it into space, remember, than have flown an HPA, so I stood on the runway at Sywell a very contented man. My legs were knackered, but not so tired that I couldn't make it off the runway to celebrate with a sip of champagne!

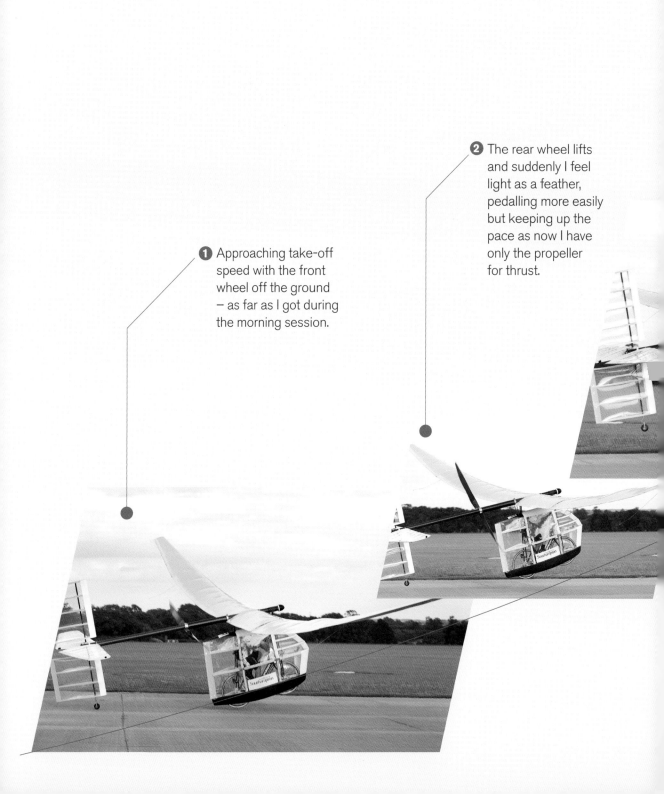

1 Approaching take-off speed with the front wheel off the ground – as far as I got during the morning session.

2 The rear wheel lifts and suddenly I feel light as a feather, pedalling more easily but keeping up the pace as now I have only the propeller for thrust.

4 Approaching my cruising altitude of 10 feet (3 metres) and grinning like an idiot, proud to be an HPA pilot at last!

3 The SUHPA continues to rise and I carry on pushing my legs as fast as they will go to keep myself airborne.

Hydro-planing Motorbike

World Hydroplaning Motorbike Distance Record	
Current record: None	
Target distance: 100 m (330 ft)	
Minimum water depth: 1m (3 ft)	
Record venue: Bala Lake, Wales	

The Challenge

'Speed, an element of danger and motorbikes – three of my favourite things!'

IT'S amazing what you can find on the internet these days, isn't it? There's a heck of a lot of rubbish out there, and that can make it difficult to find the good stuff, but if you look hard enough you can always find a few gems sparkling among the dross. For obvious reasons, I tend to focus on anything to do with motorbikes, and that's what led me to some video clips of blokes in Argentina and in the United States riding their dirt bikes across ponds and lakes.

They weren't riding the bikes across the bottoms of the ponds – they were skimming right across the surface. Some of the ponds they were riding across didn't look too deep but, even so, motorbikes – even dirt bikes – aren't designed to float across water. Dirt bikes may be in their element off road, but 'off road' doesn't usually mean 'off hard ground altogether'! On a couple of the clips you could see a bloke standing in the pond as the bikes shot past and he was just about up to his backside in water, so there was plenty of depth available for the bikes to do just what you would expect – sink like stones. Yet they managed to stay upright and keep going.

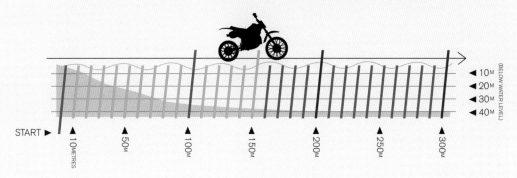

The bikes didn't look like they had been modified with floats or anything like that – I would have spotted that straight away – and they looked like they were running on normal knobbly tyres for charging around on loose surfaces. So how were they managing to ride across water?

Admittedly, in most of the clips that I saw, the riders were only on the water for around five seconds or so, but that is more than enough time to sink a motorbike. Some of the riders were more successful than others, with a fair few losing their bikes and doing involuntary acrobatics over the handlebars. Luckily most looked like they walked away pretty much unhurt ...

Anything that goes wrong on a motorbike when you've built up a bit of speed is bad news for the rider.

The fact that it was clearly a bit risky was the clincher for me. If all of the clips had made it look like anybody could ride a motorbike on water, then I wouldn't have been so interested, but the ones who didn't get it quite right and paid the price showed that there was an element of danger involved. There had to be, really, because they were all cracking on at a fair pace when they reached the water's edge, and anything that goes wrong on a motorbike when you've built up a bit of speed is bad news for the rider.

So, here was something that involved speed, an element of danger, and motorbikes – three of my favourite things! What I had to do was to find out how they were managing the water biking stunt and whether there was any kind of

Below: Normally our bike would have been quite happy on ordinary off-road tyres, but off-road and on-water are two different things!

Above: The Osprey team's rescue boats at Bala Lake were there to recover both me and the bike from the water – in that order.

official record for it. It didn't look to me like the lads in the videos were covering a huge distance on the water, and there had to be a reason for that, otherwise people would be riding bikes around on reservoirs and canals all over Britain. If there was a record for time or distance, I would have a target to aim for, and all I would need then would be a suitable bike, a big enough pond, and someone to explain to me what the heck was going on!

Discovering the World of Hydroplaning

To find out how a motorbike could cross a pond, I needed some advice from someone who knew a lot more than I did about sending things hurtling across water.

SKIMMING stones was about my limit, but even with that I could see that there were forces and techniques involved that I would have to get to grips with. Chuck any old stone on to the surface of the water and it will make a splash, but it will go straight to the bottom. On the other hand, I knew that if you picked up a flat stone, got down really low and threw it out across the water, it would glance off the water and skip across the surface, especially if it left your hand spinning like a discus. What was going on there, then?

The man with the answers was Dr Hugh Hunt, a fellow of Trinity College, Cambridge. Among his many other achievements, in 2011 Hugh was the engineer who recreated Barnes Wallis's bouncing bomb, the one used by the Dambusters during the Second World War, for a TV show demonstrating how Wallis developed the idea. Hugh successfully skimmed his version of the bouncing bomb across a lake in Canada to blow up a dam that they had built specially for the show. It didn't sound quite the same thing as riding a motorbike across a pond, and I really didn't want any effort that I made to end with a massive explosion, but Hugh was able to explain what was going on with the motorbikes that rode on water.

Basically, what the riders were doing was hydroplaning. This is something anyone who drives on the open road in any kind of truck, car or motorbike has probably heard about, even if they don't know exactly how it works. I knew that something as big as a truck could quickly become uncontrollable if it hit a patch of standing water on the road. The wheels no longer have any traction and the vehicle drifts, as though it's floating. It can happen to anyone driving too fast over a wet surface and it's not something you'd normally want to experience, but the guys on those internet videos appeared to be having fun mastering the art of hydroplaning. In the few seconds they spent skimming across the water, they were also achieving respectable distances – so I made some enquiries about what the world record was for hydroplaning. I got in touch with the people at Guinness World Records and quickly discovered that there was no official record.

Hydroplaning is all to do with a build-up of water pressure beneath the wheels.

Now I had a challenge on my hands and they gave me some guidelines about what I would have to do to set a record. They insisted that I would have to use a standard motorbike that could not be modified in order to make it float. I could add foils or planes (more about them a little later) to the bike to help it hydroplane, but they were adamant that the 'modifications must not affect the static buoyancy of the motorcycle' so that 'if the motorcycle comes to a stop it MUST NOT float'. They also specified a minimum depth of 1 metre (3 feet) over the length of the course. That all sounded fine to me, and Hugh confirmed that, if we got it all right, in theory I could hydroplane as far as I liked until the fuel tank ran dry. Once I was on the water, it would all depend on achieving a perfect balance between the thrust from the rear wheel and the drag generated by my progress through the water.

Now things were starting to sound a bit familiar. Hydroplaning is all to do with a build-up of water pressure beneath the wheels. We've seen in the previous chapters the effect that air pressure can have, especially in generating lift when it flows over a wing. As a fluid, water behaves in much the same way that air does, and marine engineers have understood this for many years. A wing, or foil, works the same way in water as it does in the air. As long ago as the 1890s, boat designers were experimenting with foils on their boats – hydrofoils – to lift the hulls of the boats out of the water. An Italian called Enrico Forlanini spent years developing his hydrofoil boat, which he tested on Lake Maggiore in 1906. The boat had two huge propellers, both mounted above the water line to operate in the air like aeroplane props, and different levels of foils attached to the hull. When the boat was at rest the hydrofoils lay in the water, but as the props powered the boat forward the hydrofoils lifted the hull clear of the water. Forlanini's boat was very quick, achieving more than 42 mph (68 km/h), making it one of the fastest boats in the world at that time.

Inventor Alexander Graham Bell, the man credited with inventing the telephone, met with Forlanini when Bell was touring the world in 1911. Bell was hugely enthusiastic about the hydrofoil concept and had sought out Forlanini to take a look at his boat. Along with his chief engineer, Casey Baldwin, Bell took a ride in

Top: Forlanini's hydrofoil rising clear of the water on Lake Maggiore in 1910.

Middle: Guy Gibson and his 'Dambusters' crew boarding their Lancaster bomber in 1943.

Bottom: The Mohne Dam after being hit by 617 Squadron's bouncing bombs.

Forlanini's hydrofoil boat on Lake Maggiore. He was so impressed with the speed and the smooth ride, the hull not being subjected to buffeting by the waves, that he and Baldwin began work on their own hydrofoil. In 1919 on the Bras d'Or Lake in Nova Scotia, Baldwin was at the controls when the Bell HD-4 hydrofoil set a new world water speed record of 70.86 mph (114.01 km/h). In more recent years, Donald Campbell set several world water speed records in his *Bluebird* hydroplane boats and made it to more than 300 mph on Coniston Water in the Lake District in 1967.

Hydrofoils are still in use today around the world, providing fast passenger ferries. Being able to lift the hull out of the water reduces the water resistance, allowing the hydrofoils to provide a fast, smooth ride for their passengers. But why were hydrofoils so important to me? I needed to know about wheels on the water, not how wings worked in water. At the end of the day it was all about pressure. Water pressure worked much the same way as I already knew air pressure to work, and it was pressure that was at the heart of the hydroplaning phenomenon. Learning a bit about hydrofoils was also to help me understand about how I could help to create the hydroplaning effect with a small but cleverly designed addition to a standard motorbike. That very special piece of kit was to come along later, Hugh still had a lot to teach me about the science of hydroplaning.

Top: Donald Campbell set seven World Water Speed records in his jet-powered hydroplane, *Bluebird*, between 1955 and 1964.

Bottom: Campbell died on Coniston Water in the Lake District when *Bluebird* rose out of the water at 300 mph and flipped over.

Top right: You have to get the angle of entry just right to be a champion stone skimmer.

Bottom right: Note the ripples caused by the stone pushing water aside, displacing the surface water and transferring some of its energy to that water, losing thrust in the process.

Keeping Your End Up

The Science of Hydroplaning

Hugh Hunt explained how Sir Isaac's First and Second Laws of Motion ruled the roost when it came to hydroplaning.

NEWTON'S First Law, remember, states that an object, whether it has parked itself in one place or is on the move, will carry on doing what it's doing unless an outside force causes the situation to change.

In the lake, the water, having gathered and been there for a while, will want to stay exactly where it is. The motorbike or, more specifically, the tyres on the motorbike (because they are first to come into contact with the water) will be moving forward at, say, 40 mph and wanting to carry on doing that. They can't both have it their own way. In fact, neither of them can.

Just as we had to consider forward thrust as a force when I was providing the thrust by pedalling Britain's Fastest Bike, and also when I was pedalling to turn the propeller in the SUHPA, we have to think about the forces that the motorbike represents. It has forward thrust provided by the engine powering its rear wheel and also the downward force of gravity. On dry land the downward force that gives the motorbike its weight helps its tyres to grip the ground, giving it traction. On water the same forces are at work. Rather than thinking about the two forces working at right angles to each other – thrust straight ahead and weight straight down – on water it is easy to see how the two forces work at an angle, slanting forwards and downwards. But the water will resist that force,

in accordance with Newton's Third Law: for every action there is an equal and opposite reaction. The water will push back on the tyre. When this happens to a vehicle on the open road it causes a huge problem. The grooves in road tyres are designed to squeeze water out from beneath the tyre, letting the tyre stay in contact with the road. When the car, truck or motorbike hits the water at speed, however, the water pushing back on the wheel creates a wedge-like bow wave of pressure in front of the tyre that pushes it up off the road. The vehicle is then skimming along on what may only be a few millimetres of water but is enough to prevent it getting any purchase on the road surface. With no traction, the driver has no control and the vehicle will go wherever the forces at work propel it.

On the road, the vehicle will carry on hydroplaning until it passes over the puddle and the tyres hit the tarmac again, or until another of our old adversaries from the previous challenges comes into play – drag. Drag in the case of a vehicle hydroplaning will be from air resistance and water resistance. If the vehicle's tyres can no longer drive it forward, drag will ultimately bring it to a halt and then gravity will be the main force acting on it, pulling it down until the wheels touch the road.

A motorbike hydroplaning across a lake has to deal with all of those forces, and keeping up the forward thrust is clearly the key to maintaining that 'Third Law' pressure that will keep the front wheel hydroplaning. And so is shifting as far back on the saddle as you can go. Hugh had no doubt that this was a major factor in achieving a successful motorbike hydroplane. The less weight there was on the front wheel, the better. The whole thing was a balancing act, balancing forward thrust against gravity and drag as well as balancing the attitude of the bike to keep the front end up on the surface.

Keeping the bike at the right angle was also going to depend on hitting the water at the right angle. The impact with the water was a crucial factor in making the bouncing bomb skim across the surface. Skimming a stone also shows you that. If you get down low in order to give the stone as flat a trajectory as possible, you get far better results. The bouncing bomb, like the skimming stone, was also spinning. The spinning gave the bomb what is called

gyroscopic stability. To try to understand how that works we have to go back to Newton's First Law again. The bomb would tend to carry on spinning at a certain angle – parallel to the surface of the water – and this helped to stop it from toppling over and going off course as it bounced on the surface.

I would have spinning wheels on my hydroplaning motorbike, of course, but because they wouldn't be spinning freely – they would be churning through the water – they wouldn't provide me with any stability. All gyroscopic bets were off in that respect. Hugh also pointed out that I would have another problem with balance when the wheels left firm ground and hit the water. Without the grip that the tyres provided on dry land, I would need to draw deep on my motorcycling experience to stay upright. He described how it would be like trying to stand on a tea tray in a room where the floor is covered with marbles. I wasn't too worried about that. If the guys on the internet could manage to stay upright, then so could I. Though I might not be too confident balancing on marbles while standing on a tea tray, give me a motorbike and I'd fancy my chances.

Lift

When the front wheel of the bike enters the water the surface water is easily displaced as spray. Just below the surface, where the water is under more pressure from the volume of water all around it, it is not so easy to displace and a wedge of high-pressure water builds up under the wheel, providing lift to counter the wheel's weight.

The planing surface uses the same kind of pressure build-up seen in the front wheel's 'wedge' to provide lift. Creating that pressure is all down to maintaining a constant thrust. If the thrust drops the bike is likely to nose dive into the lake.

Drag

→
→
→

Thrust

←
←
←

Lift

The part of the wheel that is out of the water (most of it once the wedge has built up) encounters our old pal air resistance, or drag. The thrust from my tyre needs to fight the air resistance and the water resistance for me to make headway, although the water resistance is also my friend in helping to provide lift.

The same forces acting on the wheel also act on me and the rest of the bike. Drag becomes a major factor as the rear wheel struggles to provide the kind of thrust that it could supply when it has traction on solid ground.

New Tricks
for a Magic Bike

Getting hold of the kind of motorbike that I would need wasn't such a problem. The nice people at Suzuki let us have one of their RM Z450 bikes.

THIS bike has won awards for being a tough and reliable off-road machine. We were amazed at just how reliable it was, despite the things we were asking it to do! The bike has a single-cylinder, 449 cc engine capable of delivering all the power I would need and accelerating quickly across rough terrain. It was a beauty, but I needed someone to help me turn it from being an award winner on dry land to a record breaker on water – and I found them in Devon.

Sealander Marine International are based in Plymouth and they are people who are used to taking things that you would think should be driving along a road, and sending them skimming across water instead. Graham Davis is a marine engineer and the Managing Director, while Charlie Broughton works with Sealander as a design engineer, developing, among other things, amphibious vehicles. Charlie designs the sort of thing that you can drive down a slipway in Southampton with 40 passengers aboard and drive out of the water on the Isle of Wight, delivering the passengers to their hotel without anyone ever getting their feet wet. If I was going to add foils or planes to the bike – always bearing in mind the Guinness directive that the bike should not float – these were the lads to turn to.

Charlie showed me an image of the Suzuki projected on to the side of a van – a rare bit of nice clean space in an otherwise busy workshop – and described how the ideal place to position what he called a 'planing surface' would be between the wheels right under the main chassis of the bike. If I got my balance right, the front wheel would take care of itself, as it did for the riders on the internet videos, and the planing surface would supply the lift required to keep me on the surface. Charlie's rough drawing looked a bit like the hull of a boat with an open rear end, which is hardly surprising because what we wanted it to do was to act like the hull of a boat. What Charlie had to concentrate on, and I would have to bear in mind when I was riding, was to get the planing

Above: The Suzuki had a relatively smooth front tyre to help the wheel skim across the water.

Right: That single-cylinder, 499 cc engine was a thing of beauty.

surface at the optimum angle to the surface of the water. Like the wing of an aircraft, the angle of attack would affect its efficiency. He reckoned that we needed it to sit up from the rear to the nose at an angle of no more than 4.5°. On a boat, any more than that and you would be wasting thrust trying to push the whole thing into the air. If you dropped too far below that, then you would be wasting thrust by ploughing the thing down into the water. Once again, we were talking about achieving the perfect balance to get maximum speed across the water from the thrust available.

If I got my balance right, the front wheel would take care of itself.

The planing surface would have to be kept as light as possible, but it would be taking a real pounding, so it also needed to be strong. Charlie planned to use aluminium for the outer surface of the plane, reinforced with aluminium spars running down each side and ribs running across the inner 'hull' like the bulkheads of a ship. The front of the plane would have to curve upwards to make sure that it didn't dig into the water and force the bike down rather than up. Instead of ending abruptly after the main body, the plane would be forked at the rear with a trailing arm running either side of the rear wheel.

Right: Charlie shows roughly where the planing surface will go and that we want a rear 'paddle' tyre.

The Perfect Tyre

On the rear wheel we would experiment with a standard 'knobbly' tyre but also try out a sand tyre. I had heard of these being fitted to bikes used on beaches or in the desert, where a normal tyre wouldn't really cut the mustard. The sand tyre doesn't have grooves cut into it like an ordinary tyre but has a dozen 'paddles' sticking out of the tread area. These push the loose sand behind the wheel to drive the bike forward and would hopefully push water behind as well, just like the paddle wheel on

Left: A sand tyre, normally used for racing on beaches or desert dunes, was what we thought would work best as a rear 'paddle' wheel.

Above: The Suzuki had a normal chain drive – simple, robust and reliable.

Below: Knobbly off-road tyres gave us a proper surprise when we tested them.

a Mississippi steamboat. It was a modification that Guinness were perfectly happy with, but we would still have to run some tests to see whether the sand tyre would produce more thrust than a more conventional off-road knobbly.

On a concrete slipway on the banks of the River Tamar, Graham and Charlie set up a rig to test the thrust we could expect from the Suzuki's rear wheel. We took off the front wheel and attached the bike's front forks to the rear of the test rig, which was set up on a boat trailer. Then we rolled the whole lot down to the water's edge so that the Suzuki's rear wheel was in the river. When I gunned the engine, the wheel would spin in the water and the thrust it produced would push the bike forwards against the test rig where a sophisticated electronic strain gauge would register how many kilograms of forward thrust we were getting. Obviously, we had set it up so that the front suspension wasn't cushioning the thrust from the wheel. What could possibly go wrong?

Actually, the fancy strain gauge could. And when a replacement was tried, that wouldn't work either. Then some bright spark said, 'Hang on. If we're measuring the thrust in kilograms, why not just use an ordinary set of bathroom scales?'

Below: The scooped ridges on the sand tyre were what made it such a good paddle wheel.

Above: Fitting the rear wheel prior to testing the tyres on the Tamar slipway.

Of course, there was nowhere thereabouts to buy a set of scales, and by now all the people on the TV crew who'd come to film the thrust test were looking at me and smiling. There were houses close by and there was probably a set of scales in every bathroom in every house. All I had to do was go and ask someone. Can you imagine someone turning up on your doorstep in the middle of the afternoon and asking to borrow your bathroom scales? The TV crew love it when I have to do something like that. I'm sure they all get together before each shoot and say, 'Right – who's got any ideas for something really stupid that we can we get Guy to do this time?' I don't really mind. They're a great bunch and it's all part of the fun. As it turned out, the gentleman in the first house that I went to was more than happy to lend us his bathroom scales, we strapped

them to the test rig and they worked just fine. Graham and Charlie had worked out that the overall weight, with me at around 75 kilograms, the bike at around 110 kilograms, and a bit added on to account for the fact that I would be soaking wet and that we were bolting extra bits to the bike, meant that the planing surface would have to generate lift of roughly 200 kilograms. For it to do that, they calculated that we would need at least 50 kilograms of thrust from the rear wheel.

We tried the knobbly tyre first, dipping it into the water to different depths to see how that affected its performance. The answer was that it could not produce a consistent performance. The best it could achieve was nowhere near what we needed, and some readings even showed the knobbly producing negative thrust – it was trying to drag me into the Tamar! We also experienced a major problem with the wheel suddenly starting to spin faster and the engine revs rising. When I backed off the throttle, I quickly found the wheel slowing down and the revs dropping too low. If this was what it was going to be like when I was attempting to hydroplane, I would never be able to maintain a steady thrust. Graham explained that what we were seeing here was cavitation.

Cavitation happens when forces acting on the water, such as those produced by a propeller or our Suzuki's rear wheel, cause rapid changes in pressure. This can lead not only to areas of high and low pressure, but also to a void forming for an instant – almost like a vacuum bubble. When the water rushes into the void it does so with enormous force, and when those tiny jets of water smash into a metal propeller they can cause pitting on the surfaces of the blades. For us, cavitation would mean the tyre tread, or the sand tyre paddles, plunging into the water as the wheel revolved and trying to push against a void, or an area of low pressure, where they would encounter little or no resistance. That would let them push through really easily, allowing the rear wheel to spin faster and causing the engine revs to shoot up. It would be like the rear wheel skidding on ice or someone burning rubber doing doughnuts on a race track – a lot of noise and energy expended without any forward thrust being generated. In short, cavitation would leave me dead in the water and I would sink.

The hope was that, in deeper water when we would have good forward momentum,

Above: We had plenty of gear with us to work out our thrust measurements – everything bar the kitchen sink . . . and the bathroom scales!

the rush of water would prevent any voids from forming and we wouldn't have a problem with cavitation. Maintaining the momentum and keeping the rear wheel at the optimum depth would help. Again, it was all coming down to balance.

Cavitation aside, it was clear that the knobbly probably wasn't going to do the job for us, so we fitted the sand tyre to the rear wheel instead. The difference was amazing. We were seeing up to 100 kilograms of thrust, more than enough for our purposes. That made the choice of rear tyre very easy and we could finally drag the test rig back up the slipway. I returned the scales to the gentleman who had kindly lent them to us. They were a lot drier than I was, but nothing could dampen my spirits at that point. I was going to rip across that water!

Right: The knobbly tyre produced a fine plume of spray but a very disappointing thrust reading.

Cavitation Effect

Cavitation can occur when an object is moving at speed in water. The leading edge of the object creates an area of high-pressure water in front of it and an area of low-pressure water in its slipstream. The water pressure in the slipstream can drop so low that the water turns to vapour. Here's a simple look at how it happens and the problems it may cause.

Thrust

The sand tyre on the Suzuki could suffer from a kind of cavitation when the ridges that are to behave like paddles in the water create high pressure in front of them as they are pushed through the water, and a low pressure 'slipstream' area immediately behind them.

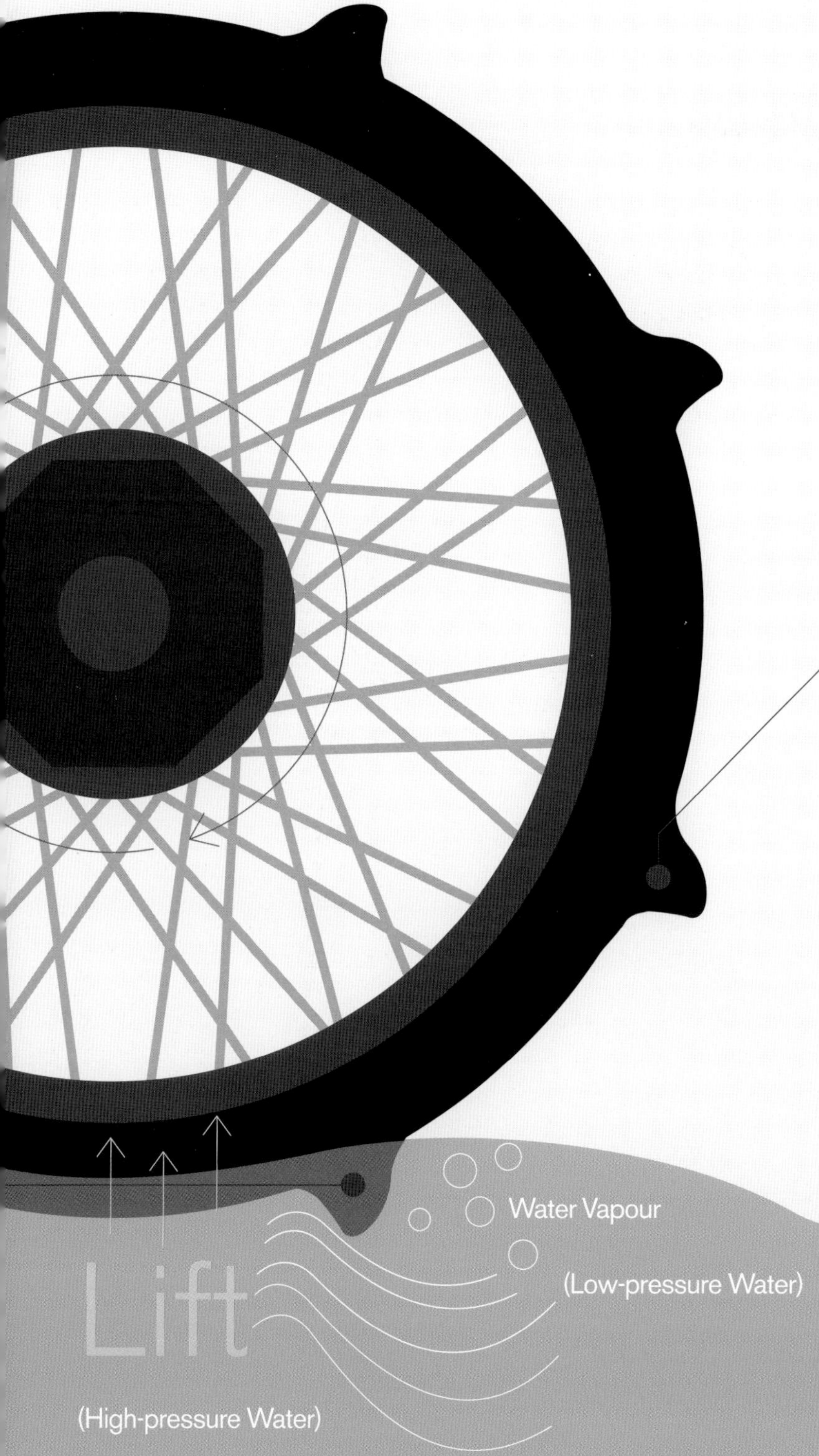

When the next ridge crashes into that low pressure area it will have less water to push on and will zip through a lot faster without actually providing as much forward thrust for the bike.

Because the bike will be moving forwards, the flow of water onto the wheel should be such that the low pressure areas will be 'filled' with the water that the wheel is heading into, making cavitation less of a problem, but I knew that if I suddenly felt the engine revs rise it would be caused by the rear wheel spinning faster, losing its 'grip' on the water. I would then, quickly but delicately, have to try to cut back the throttle then gently build it up again. Dealing with cavitation would need split-second timing and a bit of good luck into the bargain.

Water Vapour

(Low-pressure Water)

Lift

(High-pressure Water)

Nature's Hydroplaning Experts

I was able to learn quite a bit about how Mother Nature had equipped some creatures to deal with the things that I had experienced in my previous challenges, so it made sense to see if there was anything to be learned from the natural world about hydroplaning.

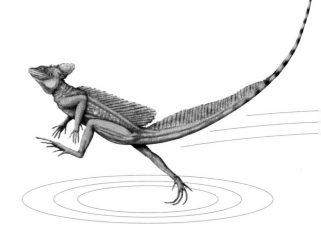

IT SEEMED highly unlikely that there would be creatures out there who were attempting to do anything like riding a motorbike across a lake, but nature is full of surprises. The first surprise was a South American creature called the basilisk lizard. The basilisk lives in the rainforests, never too far away from water, and if it thinks something is sneaking up on it the lizard sprints off towards the nearest water – and just keeps going. It runs across the surface on its hind legs with most of the rest of its body out of the water. Now you're probably thinking that the basilisk runs on water because it's only about the size of a fingernail, but these guys can actually grow reasonably large. An adult male can be up to 80 cm (2 feet 8 inches) long, although 75 per cent of that will be its tail. Nevertheless, they are specially equipped for running on water. They have large hind feet with scaly flaps on the long toes. On land these are folded tight to the toes, but when it takes to the water they fan out, giving the feet a larger surface area. When it runs on water the basilisk slaps its feet down on to the surface, pushing water out to the side, trapping bubbles of air and also creating downward pressure that is countered by the water. It then pushes its foot back to paddle forwards and keep up its

momentum before that foot is lifted and the other one slaps down.

Smaller, lighter basilisks can manage greater distances across the water before they eventually start to sink, but they are all good swimmers and can even stay underwater for up to an hour, making the nearest river or pond a real safe haven for them. Their ability to walk on water, albeit only for a short burst, has led them to become known as the Jesus lizard.

Although it is using some of the principles involved in hydroplaning, thrust and pressure, the Jesus lizard hasn't really mastered hydroplaning as well as aquatic birds like the swan. If you ever catch a glimpse of a swan coming into land on water you will see a real hydroplaning expert at work. Having stalled its wings – I know quite a bit about that from my glider experience – the swan extends its legs forward towards the water and spreads its webbed feet at exactly the right angle of attack to allow it to hydroplane across the surface until its forward momentum is exhausted and it can settle gently on to the pond. The whole landing sequence means that the swan, and other aquatic birds, can come in for a controlled landing rather than simply smashing

down into the water at high speed. That's not a comfortable experience, as I was to discover for myself when we started running the Suzuki into a lake!

The other of Mother Nature's marvels that has been seen indulging in a spot of hydroplaning is the dolphin. It seems to me like these guys will do anything for a bit of fun, but there's a serious side to their high-speed capers. Fish will sometimes swim into really shallow water at the very edge of a beach rather than become a dolphin's dinner. The dolphins, being so much bigger, can't manoeuvre in water that's only a few centimetres deep. Their forward thrust is generated by pumping their tails up and down in the water and they need a reasonable depth of water to do that. Rather than let a good fish supper get away, however, some dolphins have figured out that if they work up enough speed they can skim into the shallows with most of their bodies out of the water, hydroplaning towards their prey. There's an element of danger involved for the dolphin, however. If he beaches himself and can't get back into deep water, he's in trouble.

You have to love that about dolphins, don't you? They seem to live for speed and danger.

I might even be tempted to think that I was a dolphin in a previous life – if I wasn't such a poor swimmer!

Above: Swans and other large aquatic birds hydroplane beautifully using their webbed feet as planing surfaces to rob them of speed as they come in to land on water.

By filming a lizard running across water that had beads floating on the surface, scientists were able to work out that the lizard has three phases to its running stride.

Second phase – the stroke. The lizard pushes backwards with its foot, using the toe flaps like paddles to push against the water. Newton told us that every action has an equal and opposite reaction, the lizard pushes water backwards, the water pushes him forwards.

First phase – the slap. The lizard smashes its foot vertically down onto the surface of the water, trapping air beneath the flaps on its toes that it has spread out. That way it can trap more air for buoyancy and spread its weight over a larger surface area, pushing down on more water to give the water the best chance to push back. Pushing down gives the lizard its lift.

Third phase – recovery. Balance is key to a successful sprint across the pond, so the lizard uses its tail to help keep him steady, but he also pushes out to the side with his foot to stop himself toppling over. As his rear foot exits the water, of course, his front foot is ready for the next slap.

When drag and weight finally overcome the lizard, he might scamper across the surface on all fours for a bit before he settles down to swim. The basilisks can swim very well and even hold their breath underwater for up to half an hour, two skills that would be quite handy for a truck mechanic trying to ride a motorbike across a lake!

Upside Down Safety Training
Getting up to Speed

Being able to cope with being dunked in water was essential for what I had to do next.

WHILE I admit that I'm no great shakes as a swimmer, I can still swim and I'm not particularly frightened of water. I understand completely why non-swimmers might be worried about paddling at the beach in water more than ankle deep, but I can cope with splashing about in water now and again, otherwise I wouldn't be quite so attracted to the thought of riding a motorbike across a lake.

There was another element to hydroplaning the motorbike that I needed to investigate and it involved the way that the planing surface would rise out of the water. Once it was out of the water, its shape would force air down towards the surface, creating a cushion of high-pressure air that it could ride on. That, at least, was the theory, and to see that theory put to the test I needed to experiment with a planing surface a bit bigger than the one we were going to use on the Suzuki. I was about to get a taste of Formula One powerboat racing. Before I could do that, however, I had to have a dunking.

In the whole of mainland Britain, you can't get much further from the sea than Burntwood in Staffordshire. Halfway between Birmingham and Stafford, just off the M6 toll road, it's slap-bang in the middle of England, so it might seem like a strange place to be teaching me anything about powerboats, but it was in the swimming pool at Chase Terrace Technology College that I was to undergo immersion testing.

Immersion testing is basically capsize training for powerboat racers, and, seeing the test rig set up at the side of the pool for the first time, I did start to wonder a bit about whether I was quite as confident in the water as I liked to think. It looked like a scary piece of kit – some sort of torture chamber, maybe – and there was a good reason for that ... it was scary and it was torture!

Before I was strapped into the test rig, however, I had to have a crash course in using breathing equipment. Yours truly, the dodgy swimmer, was about to be trained as a scuba diver – and it wasn't at all bad. The training was really pretty basic and intended just to get me used to breathing through a mouthpiece and swimming

---

Below: I've never been a great swimmer, but I was getting to quite enjoy the scuba diving lark in the pool at Chase Terrace Technology College.

Top right: The 'torture chamber' rig, a mock-up of a Formula One powerboat cockpit, was explained to me in great detail.

Bottom right: The framework allowed the entire cockpit to be turned upside down to simulate a crash.

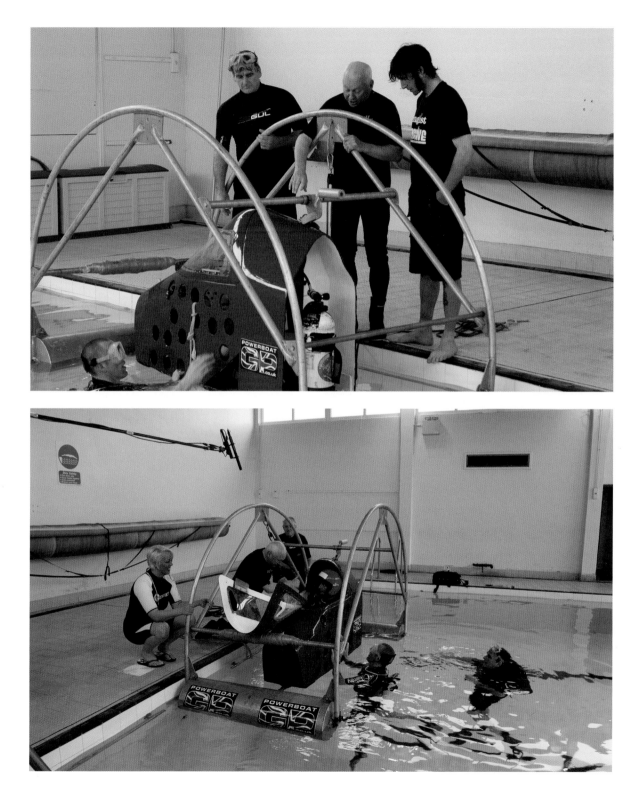

underwater with the air tank strapped to my back. There was someone with me all the way, but I quite enjoyed drifting around under water in the pool. It was quiet and peaceful, any sounds being muffled by the water, and I was far more relaxed than I expected to be. You can't talk underwater with a mouthpiece in place, so I had to learn the hand signals – making a circle with your thumb and forefinger to signal 'OK', for example. A thumbs-up signal doesn't mean 'good' or 'OK', it means, 'I want to go up,' and thumbs down means the opposite. It was all quite logical, and by the time we had to leave the scuba stage behind I was starting to enjoy being a diver. Now, however, it was time for the torture rig.

They say that drowning is a peaceful way to go, but that doesn't seem right to my way of thinking. Panic and fear don't really sit well alongside peaceful, do they? The test rig was designed to teach powerboat drivers their escape drill should their boat capsize in the water, and if there's anything that can take the edge off panic, it's good training. These boats, you see, have enclosed cockpits. From the outside they look as much like spaceships as they do boats, with the driver sealed inside his cockpit. The test rig holds a powerboat cockpit in a framework that allows it to be tipped upside down in the water, simulating a crash where the boat has capsized. If I was to be allowed in a Formula One boat, I had to be able to master the evacuation procedure.

I was strapped into the driver's seat and then, just like on a Formula One racing car, the steering wheel was handed to me so that I could slot it on to the steering column. There

were only three things to remember – pull the tab to release the canopy, remove the steering wheel, unclip my safety harness. Canopy. Steering wheel. Harness. Then I could wriggle out of the cockpit and make for the surface. The important thing was not to panic and to let the boat settle before I started trying to evacuate.

After a couple of dry runs, it was time for a very wet one. The canopy was put in place, I signalled that I was good to go, and in the blink of an eye the whole cockpit was suddenly upside down and filling with water! It comes as a real shock when you're warm and dry one moment and the next you are upside down, drenched, and water is shooting up your nose! I stayed calm, followed the procedure and was out of the cockpit in no time, with two divers on hand to make sure I was OK.

Then we did it again, I waited a second for the cockpit to stop rocking ... then canopy, steering wheel, harness. I groped my way out and the divers were right there to help. There was great visibility in the pool, but I had to remember, on a lake where the silt on the bottom had been churned up by the powerboat's propeller, it would be as dark as night.

The divers, and the blokes training me on the rig, were from Osprey Powerboat Rescue. They follow the Formula One boats all over the world from the UK to South America and the Far East, and their divers will be at the site of a crash within seconds to help get the driver out. They would be on hand when I got behind the wheel of a real powerboat, and when I took to the water on the Suzuki. You've no idea how reassuring it was for me to have the Osprey team on board.

Left: Canopy, steering wheel, harness – that's all I had to remember, but it seemed like a lot at the time!

Flying Across the Water

Burntwood may have seemed like a crazy place to be doing capsize training, but there was method in our madness as it is only a stone's throw from where I would be test driving the powerboat.

T HE 200-acre Chasewater Reservoir was created in 1797 to help feed Birmingham's 160-mile-long canal network. In those days the canals were an integral part of Britain's transport system and industrial hinterland, and keeping them topped up was vital. By the twentieth century the growth of the railway network along with the speed and convenience of road transport meant that the canals took a back seat, and Chasewater began to be developed for leisure use. In 1958 it became home to the South Staffordshire Hydroplane and Speedboat Club, and regular race meetings were held there. It quickly grew in popularity for racing, with major international events being staged on the reservoir, including 24-hour races that turned Chasewater into the Le Mans of the powerboat world! Unfortunately, falling water levels caused by seepage through the dams that were built more than 200 years ago to create Chasewater led to it becoming too shallow for the powerboats, and other water sports came to dominate the reservoir – until we came along.

In 2012 a two-year programme of major remedial work on the dams was completed and the water started to rise back to its old level. They are hopeful that powerboat racing will return to Chasewater, but in the meantime our hydroplaning team gathered there to meet Jonathan Jones, four times Formula One Powerboat World Champion, and inspect his powerboat racer. Jonathan had raced at Chasewater many times during his career, and although he is now retired from racing he is still very much involved in the sport. Jonathan set up Dragon Powerboats in 2005, designing and building these fantastic machines along with engineer David Morgan.

With its spaceship styling, the Dragon F1 boat looked pretty fast, but how fast was it really? Jonathan was the man with the answers. 'It will do over 160 mph,' he said, 'and 0–60 mph in 2 seconds.' That's fast. I could hardly believe it. I ride racing motorbikes that would be doing well if they could post speed and acceleration figures like that. I said something to Jonathan about the boat being as quick as a Formula One car and he just smiled. 'I raced a Formula One car a few years ago,' he said. 'We were in London's Docklands at the City Airport. We had the car on the runway and I was on the water. There were traffic lights set up to start us and we had a quarter-mile drag race. It was close – a photo finish – but I beat the car.'

I knew that Jonathan wasn't having me on, but it was still difficult to imagine travelling at speeds like that on water – then he started talking about how they achieved them and it all started to make sense. The boat has a 2.5-litre Mercury outboard motor that is specially tuned to produce 400 horsepower – that's more power than a modern Porsche Carrera sports car, and in a vehicle that, at no more than 500 kilograms with the driver on board, is only one third of the Porsche's weight.

Yet, while a Porsche runs on fat tyres to give it maximum grip on the road, the Dragon has what looks like a remarkably small propeller to push it through the water. Jonathan explained

that when it gets up to speed, the twin hulls, or sponsons, are designed to rise up out of the water, hydroplaning until only about 5 centimetres (2 inches) of the boat are actually in contact with the water. The catamaran-style twin hulls trap air beneath them, riding on an air cushion that minimises drag to let the Dragon accelerate like a bullet and hit that remarkable top speed of 160 mph plus. What we were hoping to do with the motorbike was to hydroplane and keep it on the surface. The Dragon boat takes it a step further, with the sponsons then using air pressure to stay out of the water. Having seen the effect that slamming through the open air could have when I was pedalling Britain's Fastest Bike and trying to get the SUHPA off the ground, it was easy to see how the Dragon boat could use the air keep it out of the water. Clearly, if the driver got a bit carried away and let the front of the boat rise too far, the whole thing would flip over

Above: Jonathan Jones perched on the Dragon as I got to grips with the controls, but he abandoned ship before I started to give it some welly.

backwards, which was something to be avoided – again, balance was the key. Since Donald Campbell, everyone involved in hydroplaning boats has known how this works. Although Campbell was using an engine from a fighter jet and, ultimately his hydroplane, the *Bluebird* did flip over, resulting in a devastating crash in which he was killed.

At Chasewater we weren't aiming for anything like the speeds that Campbell had achieved, but still the Dragon would be going so fast that, if you were driving along the M6 motorway at the legal limit of 70 mph and the central reservation was a canal, it would come past you like you were going backwards. I could

Above: 'Only one careful owner, sir – a nun who only used it to go shopping.' I would have bought it on the spot after the test drive I'd just had.

hardly believe he was going to let me have a go and couldn't wait to climb into the cockpit – but, needless to say, driving one of these boats wasn't as simple as parking your backside in the driving seat of my old Astra van.

Jonathan showed me how the buttons on the steering wheel and on the floor could be used to alter the angle and depth of the Mercury motor, the angle of the propeller and the way the power was delivered, determining how the twin hulls rose out of the water. I would be able to control the throttle as well, but there were no brakes, and when the sponsons were out of the water there wouldn't be much steering available, either! To go round corners I would have to ease back on the throttle to allow the hulls to drop down into the water. Then the outboard could be used to turn the boat. Jonathan took the boat out on to the reservoir, running it round a basic oval circuit between two buoys. The cornering looked impossibly quick, the engine noise was amazing and the sight of the Dragon streaking across the reservoir while sitting up on its tail was incredible. All I wanted him to do was bring it back to the slipway so that I could have a go!

When I finally got the chance to squeeze into the cockpit, there was a familiar feeling about the 'unfinished' appearance. Like Dave Jenkins's racing truck or Guy Westgate's glider, the smooth, glossy finish on the outside disguised a far from glossy interior. Like all racing machines, there were no creature comforts or decorations, just the basic controls and instruments needed. Nothing fancy, just the tools you want to get on with the job. I like that.

Steering the boat away from the dock, I could feel every ripple of the water punching the hull. There was none of the suspension you would have on a car or a motorbike to iron out the bumps. It was more like riding a soap-box cart down a cobbled street. Building up speed, the buffeting was even more violent, with harder thumps coming less frequently as the sponsons smashed through the waves. Then, as if by magic, the sponsons rose clear of the water, the noise levels dropped dramatically and the ride was suddenly very smooth. I had that cushion of air beneath me and I was flying across the surface of Chasewater.

The buoy where I had to turn was in my sights in no time at all. I couldn't use all of the controls that Jonathan did to move the outboard up, down, forwards or backwards – I had to be content with easing back on the throttle. It had the same effect in that the twin hulls dropped down into the water, and when I turned the wheel to round the buoy the boat reacted like a whiplash. I had never felt anything like it. I turned through 180° – a full about turn – in a fraction of a second. Nothing I had ever ridden or driven on dry land, whatever the tyres or the road surface, had ever reacted like that. In turns, F1 powerboat drivers have to cope with huge g-forces in the turns (anything up to about 6.5g). That's more than a Spitfire pilot experienced in a tight turn during the Battle of Britain – and they used to black out.

Turning a vehicle at speed produces centrifugal force that throws the occupants to the outside of the turn, just as being on a spinning roundabout will tend to push you to its outer edge. A Spitfire pilot's head, because he had banked the aircraft to make it turn, was closer to the turning circle than his feet, so the centrifugal force sent the blood from his upper body outwards towards his feet, starving his brain of oxygen and causing him to black out for an instant until the aeroplane levelled out.

Fortunately for me, the Dragon boat didn't bank into the turn, so the blood wasn't drained from my head, although I was slammed against the side of the cockpit and was grateful for the crash helmet I was wearing. The turn was also completed far more quickly than the banking turn of a Spitfire, so my body really had no time to react to the immense g-force I was experiencing. Safe to say it fairly took my breath away and left me with a whopping great grin on my face! Round the buoy, power on and I was quickly floating on air again. What a machine! I really didn't want to have to hand it back …

Watching from dry land, the Sealander lads were enjoying the spectacle. When I joined them for a chat, Graham pointed out that, while Charlie's design for the planing surface would do its best to lift the Suzuki out of the water, I wasn't going to be as aerodynamic as the sleek Dragon boat. The air cushion effect, if it could be achieved at all with such a small planing surface on the Suzuki, would be minimal – but I would hopefully feel that ultra-smooth ride effect when it was all working according to plan.

Building a Record Breaker

Now that I knew a good deal more about how and why hydroplaning happens, it was time to introduce our planing surface to our Suzuki.

CHARLIE had created a 3-D computer model of the planing surface and mated it to a 3-D computer model of the bike to see where best to attach it. He was making sure that his design was millimetre perfect. As he put it, 'Five minutes putting right a mistake at the design stage could save five hours trying to fix the same thing in the workshop.' I was reminded of what my old boss used to say: 'Measure twice, cut once.' Clearly, the same thing applied for design engineers working with computers. Charlie agreed, then laughed and said: 'But it's still not always a good idea for a designer to be hanging around a workshop when they're trying to put together something you've designed!'

The 3-D model was all very well, but to see how it would work on the actual bike Graham and Charlie made a template of our planing surface out of cardboard to try it against the bike. At Rattery in Devon, just outside Torquay, we got together with fabrication engineer Dave Main and welder Richard Mumford to turn Charlie's design into an actual metal object. Using the cardboard template at Richard's workshop, it was clear how the planing surface was going

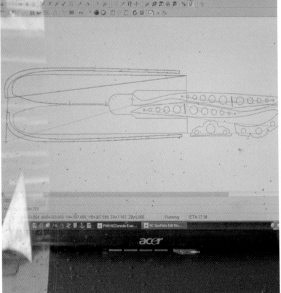

Top: Component parts for the planing surface cut from a sheet of aluminium, along with some welding rods.

Bottom: Electronic CAD drawings supplied by Charlie were loaded into the incredible water jet machine.

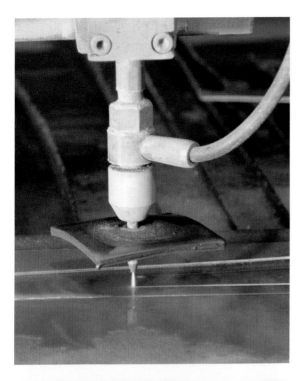

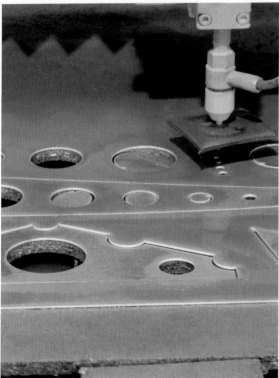

to sit like a curved shield under the Suzuki's chassis. Charlie had turned his 3-D model into a series of 2-D blueprints that would allow the individual parts of the planing surface to be cut from sheets of aluminium. The cutting process was a joy to behold.

> If you think the power jet that you use to blast the surface dirt off your patio is a mean piece of kit, then you should see this thing in action.

At Western Waterjet, not far from Richard's workshop, they have a machine that uses a massively powerful jet of water to cut through metal. If you think the power jet that you use to blast the surface dirt off your patio is a mean piece of kit, then you should see this thing in action. The concentrated jet of water can cut through six inches of steel. That would make a right mess of your patio. The cutting jet is also incredibly precise, accurate to a fraction of a millimetre and, unlike a laser, it doesn't cause the metal to get hot. Heat can make the edge that has been cut a bit brittle or distorted and difficult to work with, but the water (which has a little bit of grit in it) leaves a clean, smooth cut.

Top: The water jet cuts fast. Sean Connery talked his way out of being cut in half by a laser in *Goldfinger* but he wouldn't have had time for that with a water jet!

Bottom: You get spot-on precision with the water jet and no distortion of the components or other heat-related problems.

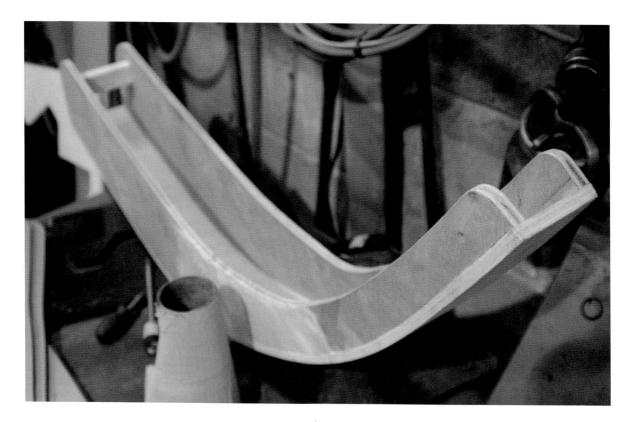

Above: A wooden form was used to help give the flat aluminium components the required curved shape.

Charlie's electronic blueprints were loaded into the waterjet's computer and the jet was then moved across the sheet of aluminium that was laid out below it. It glided over the surface like a computer-controlled dancer, cutting, stopping, moving on and cutting again. It worked like magic and the end result was spot on – a complete set of aluminium parts, like a metal Airfix kit ready for us to build into our planing surface.

The flat metal that would form the 'hull' of our planing surface had to be shaped using a forming tool to give it the curves that would let it sweep up to its bow, just like one of the F1 boat's sponsons. The shape was then reinforced by the bracing members that ran down the sides, along with the cross-member 'bulkheads'. I lent Richard a hand with the welding and, after a lot of hard graft from Richard and Dave, the planing surface emerged. There was a slight change of plan (Graham and Charlie did actually hang around for the moment of truth) when it came to exactly where the brackets would attach the planing surface to the chassis, and I used Richard's milling machine to shave a few millimetres off the mounting brackets – all proper workshop engineering. Brilliant stuff.

Right: Gathering the components together once they had been cut by the water jet.

Following page: Richard kept a close eye on me when we started welding the planing surface 'construction kit' together.

With the planing surface in place on the Suzuki, I climbed up on to the workbench and bounced around in the saddle to make sure that the suspension wouldn't cause the planing surface to smash into the ground when I was riding the bike on dry land. A few little adjustments, and we were ready to try it out.

Left: Examining the amazing job that the water jet had done on one of the bracing members.

Right: The finished planing surface awaiting a coat of paint.

Below: Deep in welding concentration with Richard overseeing.

Who's Got the Big Hammer?
Testing and Modifying

Keeping everything local, we got permission to test the bike on farmland close to the workshop.

THERE was a pond nearby, but there was no run-up and it wasn't really suitable, so we dug a trench about 50 metres long and lined it with plastic sheeting. Then we pumped some water from the pond, giving us a few centimetres in the trench. It was deepest towards the middle in order to help give me a nice, shallow entry on the bike.

Hugh Hunt was on hand to show me why the angle of entry was so important, and together we rolled spinning toy wheels down a piece of gutter pipe to see which type of tyre might best skim the surface and what angle the pipe needed to be in order to send the wheel furthest up the trench before it sank. Basically, we proved what we already knew – we needed a tyre that would maintain thrust by paddling through the water and we needed as flat an entry angle as possible. If the front wheel hit the water coming in too steep, it would plough straight in. I might get a bit of a bounce, like one of Barnes Wallis's bombs, but the bike would start doing what Graham Davis described as 'porpoising', bouncing out of the water as lift was generated by the planing surface, but then smashing back down again. Each downward splosh would rob me of forward thrust and I would struggle to stay in control. Balancing the throttle to try to keep moving forward would be impossible with the rear wheel bobbing in and out of the water.

Above: Attempting to kick-start the Suzuki after it had been dried out following one of its trips to the bottom of the lake.

The blokes on the internet videos had found out all of this by trial and error. They quickly realised that they needed a smooth, flat entry into the water and that they needed as long a run-up as they could get in order to hit the water at pace. Once I had climbed into my old racing leathers and given the Suzuki a couple of runs on the grass down the length of the trench to warm her up, I started to wonder if we had allowed enough of a run-up for me to build up speed. Graham reckoned I needed to be doing around 45 mph, and the Suzuki was no slouch, but what gear should I be in when I hit the water to make sure that the rear wheel was turning at the right speed? Graham reckoned that we were now into the 'trial and error' phase ourselves, 'one third science, one third black arts – and the rest is up to you!'

Above: Would everything that we learnt at the testing trench in Devon pay off on the record attempt?

From the far end of my run-up I could barely see the entrance to the trench. I was feeling a bit nervous. I knew I had the confidence to hold the bike flat out to build up the speed before hitting the water, but what would happen then? There would be a lot of spray – and there were power lines on electricity pylons running high above the trench. The spray wouldn't go that high, would it? I started to sense a slight whiff of hospital ...

On the first run, I gunned the engine and entered the trench in second gear. There was a lot of spray and a very slight floating feeling before the water sloshing around in the trench threw me off balance and I clipped the side wall. No damage, no injuries, but after a discussion with the team they reckoned I needed to be going faster and to have my weight a bit further back. I went again.

On the second run, I could definitely feel a bit of an hydroplane happening, the engine revs were rising as the rear wheel paddled through the water, and I had to ease off the throttle to try to achieve the balance that I needed. One of the problems seemed to be that the water in the trench wasn't really deep enough and the wheels were bouncing on the plastic sheeting.

Above: Checking the bolts on the planing surface's mounting brackets, which stood up to far more punishment than they were designed to take.

We kept at it and then Charlie decided that we might stand a better chance if we adjusted the planing surface's angle of attack slightly. Working at the edge of the trench in the sunshine, I helped the lads unbolt the planing surface from the bike but, to get it to sit exactly as Charlie wanted it, after all of that precision engineering, in the end it came down to using what is often called the 'universal adjustment tool' – a big hammer!

Once Charlie was happy with the planing surface, I stuck my helmet back on and, while the TV crew got themselves into position, Hugh Hunt fed me crisps through the bottom of the helmet – it's not easy having a snack when you're wearing a full-face motorcycle helmet. With everybody ready, I kicked the bike into life and rumbled up to the start point. This time I went for it flat out, and when I hit the water I went from juddering across the field to a sudden, smooth glide along the surface of the trench. I had time to ease back on the throttle and maintained the hydroplane right up to the end of the trench. Now we knew that, under the right circumstances, our Suzuki could hydroplane beautifully. It was a grand way to end the afternoon.

Below: The Osprey divers deliver the Suzuki ready for it to be stripped down and drained again to get the lake out of its innards.

Right: Even when I was soaking wet after being ducked in the lake, I couldn't resist helping to strip down the bike.

The Moment of Truth

When we arrived at Bala Lake in north Wales there was a lot of work to be done in preparation for the record attempt.

SET in beautiful wooded countryside and surrounded by hills, is a cracking place and a very popular holiday spot, especially with water sports enthusiasts. The lake is 4 miles (6.4 kilometres) long and a mile (1.6 kilometres) wide and was the largest natural lake in Wales until Thomas Telford raised the water level in 1797 to help control the water flow to the new Ellesmere Canal, leaving Bala still the largest lake but no longer entirely as nature intended.

When we arrived in the second week in September the area was a bit quieter than it had been over the summer, with the kids having gone back to school, and the fantastic summer that we'd had was starting to feel like a distant memory. Still, the weather was kind to us and we were able to get to work.

On our first day there, a team of local carpenters began building a wooden ramp that I could use to ride the Suzuki into the lake. We needed the ramp because the shores around the lake, even where artificial beaches had been created as landing stages for people using sailing boats or kayaks, were too steep for our purposes. That had been a major problem for us in finding somewhere that was suitable for our record attempt. At other places we looked at where there might have been a suitable entry point into a suitably calm stretch of water, getting permission to stage the record attempt proved difficult. You can imagine the sort

Above: When we tipped the bike up after it had been in the lake, water came pouring out of the exhaust pipe.

of reactions that we got when we explained that we wanted to ride a motorbike as fast as possible into the water and skim it across the surface while filming it all for the telly – 'You must be nuts, mate. You'll kill yourself. You can't do that here.'

In fact, there were genuine health and safety issues to be addressed everywhere we thought might be suitable, but at Bala, with a lot of local help, including from Bala Sailing Club, we managed to iron out all of the problems. Our sole concern now was getting the angle of entry just right, which was why the ramp was being constructed at the Pant Yr Onnen campsite on the south side of the lake.

While that was going on, we were able to tackle a few issues that we had to deal with at the north end of the lake. We had to see how well I would float wearing motorcycle leathers and a helmet, and the answer, if I lay back in the water, was 'very well indeed'. The Osprey lads practised hauling me out of the water and we even had a few trial runs with the Suzuki. Even though the angle of entry was all wrong, I managed to hydroplane for around 40 metres and Osprey got to grips with recovering a very wet Suzuki from the lake. The water here, however, was only about waist deep – not deep enough for the record attempt – and Guinness really wanted us to do at least 100 metres to establish a proper record.

To that end, surveyor Mike Hopkins from Storm Geomatics was out on the water with an echo sounder measuring the depth of the lake and positioning buoys using GPS and a laser theodolite to mark out the run I would take from the Pant Yr Onnen shoreline. Mike was also working out where he needed to place his equipment to measure exactly how far I managed to get on the record run.

While I was practising dunking myself in Bala Lake and sitting around in wet leathers, Graham, Charlie, Dave and Richard were practising emptying water out of the bike. I suppose that I should have sat and had a mug of tea while all this was going on, but I couldn't really do that while they were taking a bike to bits, could I? Believe it or not, we could strip the bike down, drain the fuel and the oil which were both contaminated with water, empty out all of the water, dry out the electrics and the filters, put the whole lot back together and replace the fuel and oil – all in less than half an hour! And with a bit of pumping on the kick-start, the Suzuki was up and running again.

Top: Sitting around in wet leathers, I could do with a nice cup of tea.

Bottom: The team getting the bike ready for the first record attempt.

Following page: The Osprey guys ferrying me back to the beach, having fished me out of Bala Lake.

Going for the Record

The following morning, with the ramp ready, we assembled at the campsite and started preparing for the record attempt.

MIKE Hopkins set up his measuring equipment just as the people from Guinness needed him to, while the Osprey crew got their boats and divers in the water ready to retrieve me and the bike – in that order! The TV crew set up their cameras, and there were mini cameras on the bike. My leathers had just about dried out and I got myself ready.

I had an extra piece of kit – a diver's knife strapped to my arm. The Suzuki had a small buoy in a container attached to the handlebars – a bit like the shopping basket on the front of a moped – and the buoy was attached to the bike by a length of thin rope. The idea was that, when the bike sank, the buoy would pop out and float to the surface to show the Osprey recovery guys exactly where it was. My knife was to help me cut myself free if I got tangled up in the rope underwater. I also had a 'dead

Top: Mike Hopkins was able to measure the distance I covered to the millimetre.

Middle: Sand tyres with their 'paddle' treads already fitted to spare rear wheels should they be needed.

Bottom: The ramp, with a sign in case I got lost . . .

Far right: I started my run-up to the ramp from way back in the woods.

Following page: Charging through the woods on the run-up.

metres

Could we set the first ever
hydroplaning motorbike record?

Above: With my weight back, the bike hydroplaned beautifully.

man's key' on a cord attached to my wrist. If I was flung off the bike, the key would be pulled out of its place on the handlebars, stopping the engine, so that I wouldn't be mauled by a spinning rear wheel if I came into contact with the bike in the water.

When we were all ready, I lined up for the first run. As with the trench, from my start point way back in the trees along the shoreline it was difficult to see the entry point to the ramp, so it had been marked with two fluorescent green plastic poles. I had a few butterflies in my tummy, not because I was worried about coming off the bike in the water – I've come off bikes under far less desirable circumstances –

but because everyone involved had put so much effort into getting us to this point and now it was all down to me. I gunned the engine and took off towards the ramp.

Coming through the trees I could see the fluorescent poles and beyond them the Osprey boats out on the water, all rushing towards me. I was sitting as far back as I could while still able to reach the clutch and kick up through the gears, and I hit the ramp doing a slight wheelie, the front wheel a few inches off the ground, then I was on the water and steaming towards the 100 metre marker buoy. I really thought I had nailed it first time, but the bike bounced, twisted sideways and I flew off over the handlebars. I had hit the ramp at well over 40 mph and when I came off the bike I was doing acrobatics at over 30 mph. At that speed water gives you a pretty hard landing – still, not

Above: Losing speed caused the front wheel to start dropping.

as hard as concrete or tarmac. The Osprey lads in the water were with me in an instant and I was helped up into the rescue boat. Then they had to find the bike. The buoy had popped out, but its cord had snapped in the crash. I had covered about 34 metres across the surface, and with the bottom of the lake dropping away from a depth of 1.5 metres, just off the end of the ramp, to about 35 metres further out, I had lost the Suzuki in about 10 metres of water. The water in Bala Lake is famously clear, but if you have a small fleet of motor boats racing around on the surface and a motorbike slamming into the lake bed, you're going to disturb a lot of silt from the bottom.

When the divers eventually located the bike they had to attach floatation bags to it and a line from the winch on the Osprey boat to haul the bike up. It all took quite a while, so I sat on the beach with the others, chatting about what we thought had gone wrong.

> As I waited at the start point, my head was buzzing, everything suddenly seemed to be perfectly clear.

Porpoising had been the problem. I needed to pile on the power while accelerating in the run-up but avoid letting the front wheel leave the ground, because when it came back down it had started that bouncing, porpoising

Above: By the time I was this low in the water …

effect that had scuppered the run. I needed to try sitting a little further forward and to hit a higher speed. The ramp was also perhaps a little too steep, so David Barratt, whose carpenters had built the ramp, lifted the end with help from a crowd of volunteers and shored it up to give me a shallower angle of entry.

When the Suzuki finally came ashore, we knew we might have a problem. At that depth the pressure would have forced water into places that it would not have gone in the shallows the day before. All we could do was strip it down and dry it out. Just half an hour later, incredibly, the Suzuki started on the first kick. We were back in business.

On the second run, as I waited at the start point, my head was buzzing with all the things that we had discussed – then, as the sand tyre's paddles gripped the earth and sent me rocketing forward, everything suddenly seemed to be perfectly clear. I hit the ramp at a good speed and the water at a good angle and sailed across the lake. For a few seconds I definitely had that 100-metre marker in my sights, but then the front wheel dropped and I was off over the handlebars again.

I knew that I had done better, and the verdict from Mike was … 64 metres. At that sort of depth, and with such poor visibility, I could pretty much have parked my house on the bottom of the lake and we wouldn't have been able to find it. The bike's buoy had deployed, in fact it had popped out while I was coming down the ramp, but it was difficult to tell from

Above: . . . I'd had it!

where we were on shore if it was still attached. By the time the bike was hauled to the surface for us to start the whole drying out process all over again, it had been in the water for almost an hour.

> By the time the bike was hauled to the surface for us to start the drying out process again, it had been in the water for almost an hour.

Sadly, we didn't get a chance of a third run, but no one was too downhearted. We had proved that we could hydroplane a motorbike for a massive 64 metres. It wasn't the 100 metres that we had been aiming for, but it had been accurately measured, so in my book that counts

as us having set a record. The whole team was keen to get back together to have another crack at it another time, perhaps in another place – and once I had peeled off the wet leathers and got a nice hot brew inside me I started to think that might not be such a bad idea ...

World's Fastest Sled

World Gravity-Powered Snow Sled Speed Record

Current record: 62 mph
Record holder: Rolf Allerdissen
Nationality: German
Record set: 2010

The Challenge

'The sniff of a record was enough to set the snowball rolling.'

SNOW. You either love it or hate it, I suppose. For some it means chaos on the roads, trains that fail to appear, childcare nightmares when the kids are sent home from school or, worse than mere inconvenience, livestock perishing on isolated farms or elderly relatives trapped in their homes, struggling to cope alone. If that's what snow means to you, then how could you possibly love it? On the other hand, when you throw back the curtains at first light and look out on a bright, fresh, clean world with a blanket of sparkling white snow covering everything in sight, it's difficult not to feel the same thrill that we all did when we were kids – snow is fun! When the weather got colder and the grown-ups started grumbling about snow being on the way, we would be waiting excitedly for the first flakes of snow to fall.

It might not be so much fun for grown-ups, but when you see kids running up the nearest hill and hurtling down on sledges of all shapes and sizes, you can't help but smile. When I was a lad we used to make do with a black bin-liner that we sat on and there were plenty of little home-made sleds out on the hill whenever it snowed. A proper wooden toboggan with

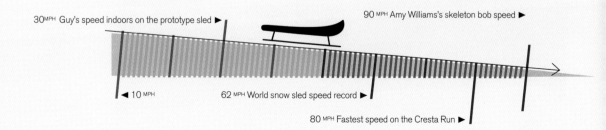

30MPH Guy's speed indoors on the prototype sled ▶

90 MPH Amy Williams's skeleton bob speed ▶

◀ 10 MPH

62 MPH World snow sled speed record ▶

80 MPH Fastest speed on the Cresta Run ▶

metal runners was an expensive piece of kit to be admired, but that was often all you could do with it, because they didn't always go as well as the bin-liners or plastic sheets, especially in deep snow. You could get up a fair speed going downhill on a plastic sheet, and that was always the appeal, especially to adrenalin junkies like me. You could be moving fast and, if you hit a bump you couldn't see or leaned the wrong way, you would end up tumbling down the slope tail over tip. A bit of speed and a bit of risk, all pretty much for free courtesy of Mother Nature. It doesn't get much better than that for a young lad, does it?

Watching kids playing in the snow on those new plastic jobs last winter, I could see that some of them were getting up a good head of steam. That set me wondering why the fancy wooden toboggans didn't always run so well and, then, just how fast can a sled go anyway? Was there a record speed, and was it something that we could maybe have a go at? I wasn't thinking about an Olympic record for something like a bobsleigh with a team of lads, or lasses, who had trained for years. What I was thinking of was a sled on an open slope, going as fast as it possibly could. Surely somebody must have done it – and it turned out somebody had ...

According to Guinness World Records, a German called Rolf Allerdissen took what they called a 'gravity powered snow sled' to just over 62 mph (about 100 km/h) on a slope in Austria in April 2010. To me that didn't sound very fast at all, and the sniff of a record was enough to set the snowball rolling.

Below: The supersled, nearing completion, looking sleek and mean.

GHIACCIO, PASTA

Warning
The Cresta Run is dangerous
Strictly private – no public access

∗∗∗

Warnung
Der Cresta Run ist Privatgrundstück –
der Zugang ist strikt untersagt

Above: Not just anyone can pop onto the Cresta Run and have a go – you have to apply and then go through the safety briefings.

Discovering the Downhill Art

I've never been a great one for winter sports. I did try snowboarding once and ended up in hospital, so before I launched myself down a hill on a gravity powered sled I reckoned I needed to find out a bit about how this sort of thing has been done in the past.

THE history of winter sports stretches back to the middle of the nineteenth century, and the British have always had a hand in it. Back in the bad old days, only the very wealthy could afford holidays. The poor working people did just that – they worked – and most wealthy people didn't really need to work at all.

For the good of their health, the rich went to the seaside. But then the railways started shipping in the less well-heeled for day trips, and the British seaside began to lose its appeal for the upper classes. British summer weather was, in any case, hardly reliable, so they started heading south for the warmth of the Mediterranean sun. They also discovered that, in the Alps, they could enjoy sunshine and fresh air at altitude as well as trying the health-giving mineral water treatments in the alpine spa towns. Visiting the spas was recommended by the medical profession for patients with chest complaints because the air was so clean and dry.

One of those towns was St Moritz, where the owner of the Kulm Hotel, Johannes Badrutt, was chatting with a handful of English gentlemen one day in the autumn of 1864 as, with the summer over, they were contemplating the long journey home. Badrutt explained to his guests that, during the winter, the mountain weather was spectacular.

He promised them that they would love the clear, fresh winter air even more than they did the summer weather. He then offered them free accommodation and guaranteed that he would pay their fares for their journeys home if they didn't enjoy the winter in St Moritz. In return, all they had to do was to tell their friends what a wonderful time they had. Badrutt knew that he would be able to tempt the English gentlemen with the kind of wager that they couldn't lose – yet it was the canny Johannes who turned out to be the winner. The Englishmen stayed for more than five months, walking in the snow-covered hills, skating on frozen lakes, enjoying sleigh rides and relaxing on the hotel terrace in the sunshine. Naturally, when Badrutt's guests travelled home in the spring with suntanned faces they raved about St Moritz, and within a couple of years the Kulm Hotel was as busy during the winter season as it was during the summer.

> The Englishmen stayed for more than five months, walking in the snow-covered hills, skating on frozen lakes, enjoying sleigh rides and relaxing on the hotel terrace in the sunshine.

Naturally the winter visitors needed to keep themselves entertained and it didn't take long for them to try tobogganing. It's a funny word, 'toboggan', isn't it? It's not really English, or even European, at all. It actually comes from the Algonquian language – the Algonquins are native Canadian people – and just means 'sledge'. Living in Canada, they used sledges for hauling their families and their belongings around throughout the long northern winter. Sledges and smaller sleds of various types were, of course, used in St Moritz during the winter as well and, just as they do everywhere, kids had their own versions to play with, and to have races with. You can probably guess that the young chaps staying in St Moritz – and the other alpine towns – quickly took to racing sleds down slopes. Being hugely competitive, they started experimenting to build their own, better, faster sleds, and that, naturally, led to racing courses being established. Building courses for toboggan racing also stopped them from causing havoc by racing through the streets of the town, which was what they had been doing!

In St Moritz, Johannes Badrutt, seizing yet another opportunity to provide a winter holiday experience that would have his guests flocking back year after year, created the first purpose-built track, carved out of the snow on the hillside with banked turns to challenge the riders' skill. This was the inspiration for the now famous Cresta Run.

The actual Cresta Run was constructed in 1884. A young Swiss geometrician named Peter Bonorad, recently returned to the area from university in Zurich, was persuaded to design the run, which was then built by a British Army officer, Major William Bulpett, along with some willing helpers and the backing of Caspar Badrutt, one of Johannes's nine children. The course ran for three-quarters of a mile (1.2 kilometres) from St Moritz to Cresta, a drop of 514 feet (157 metres), and included ten turns. It was hugely popular, but the daring young men who wanted to go as fast as possible began having problems when the banks of snow that lined the turns started to get carved up by the

Top: Sir Henry Lunn, doctor, missionary and winter sports enthusiast.

Bottom: Winter sports really started to take off after the Second World War. These Polish skiers are at Zakopane in the 1950s.

runners on the sleds. Some bright spark then decided that the answer was to spray water on the snow in the evening, which would freeze overnight, turning the snow course into a rock-hard, super-slippery ice track. The Cresta Run daredevils then became the fastest men on earth! They could hit speeds of over 60 mph at a time when there were still no cars or motorbikes, and trains were struggling to reach just 50 mph.

When most of us think of winter sports, the image that pops into our heads is of skiers, and the British have played a big part in turning skiing not only into a sport but into a major tourist industry. In places like Russia and Norway, cave paintings have been discovered that show men on skis, which means that humans have been strapping planks of wood to their feet to help them get around on snow for an incredible 7,000 years. The idea of skiing as a sport didn't come along until far more recently, and it was in Scandinavia that the first competitions evolved, although the world's first alpine ski club (alpine is downhill as opposed to cross-country skiing) was actually formed in Australia. Norwegian miners brought skiing to Kianra in the Snowy Mountains in New South Wales in 1861.

It was in European alpine resorts, however, where skiing became a major tourist attraction, and one of the key figures in its development was Sir Henry Lunn. A Lincolnshire lad, Henry became a doctor and was a missionary in India before he began organising trips to the Alps for religious conferences in the 1890s. The delegates were encouraged to take part in healthy sporting activities such as skiing, and Henry offered the services of ski instructors as part of the holiday package. He went on to form a travel agency (eventually to become Lunn Poly) and put in a lot of hard

Top: The thin runners on this toboggan from the 1950s really needed hard-packed snow or ice to work best.

Bottom: Messing around on sleds in Canada in the 1870s looks like fun but it would have been slow going given the drag that the curled front would create.

graft to develop the winter sports industry, persuading mountain railway companies across the Alps that they should remain operational throughout the winter, and doing the same with hotel owners to make sure his clients had places to stay.

But why should I be so interested in skiing? What I was looking to do, after all, was to set a world record on a sled, not on skis. It's not quite as simple as that. Skis, you see, can travel very fast indeed – and we'll be looking at the reasons why they go so fast. Sir Henry Lunn and his chums might have been slithering around on nicely carved timber planks, but modern skis are marvels of technology, and considerably

> But why should I be so interested in skiing? What I was looking to do, after all, was to set a world record on a sled, not on skis.

faster than the type of sled used in St Moritz. Whereas a champion rider on the Cresta Run today might hit a maximum speed of 80 mph, a downhill ski racer can get up to 90 mph, and a speed skier, heading straight down a slope and going for outright speed, can do 125 mph.

That is one of the reasons why Rolf Allerdissen chose to use skis, not runners, on the bottom of his sled when he set his record on the Pitztal Glacier in 2010. Clever chap. I was going to have to do the same. Skis rather than runners were obviously going to be better on snow, but, thinking back again to those proper wooden toboggans that didn't always go as fast on a slope as a boy with his bum on a bin-bag, I began to wonder why. Well, I needed a scientist to answer that one.

Above: The techniques used by riders on the Cresta Run to transfer their weight for cornering haven't really changed since these photos were taken in the 1950s.

Frost and Friction

The Science of Skiing

The team at the Centre for Sports Engineering Research (CSER) at Sheffield Hallam University were just the people to explain a few things to me about sliding down slippery slopes.

THE team at Sheffield have been involved in major sports of all sorts from badminton, golf and cycling to cricket, pistol shooting and – the skeleton bob. They designed and constructed a range of test rigs and tools to evaluate the performance of the famous Blackroc skeleton bob that Amy Williams rode to a gold medal in Vancouver at the 2010 Winter Olympics. It was Britain's only medal at the games, and a huge achievement for everyone concerned. Nick Hamilton, a principal research fellow at CSER and Senior Sports Engineer seemed like the sort of man I should be talking to.

The first thing that we had to bear in mind was that we would be going for speed on snow, not on ice, and, although ice and snow are both essentially frozen water, they are entirely different creatures. Solid ice, the sort that you make in cubes in your freezer compartment at home, forms when the temperature of a large amount of water – a large amount being anything from a single compartment in your ice cube tray to a puddle or a lake – falls below 0° Celsius. Solid ice has a crystal structure that occurs when the molecules in the water rearrange themselves into a kind of framework. In this form they are further apart than before the water froze, so water is one of the few substances that expand when they freeze. Most things contract when they reach their freezing

point. The fact that it expands means that ice is not as dense as water, which is why ice floats. Snow is also frozen water, but it forms in a slightly different way. Instead of freezing as a large mass of water, snowflakes form when a tiny droplet of moisture in the air freezes, usually freezing to a dust particle which becomes the nucleus of the snowflake. More droplets freeze on to the original one and the snowflake, which is a kind of ice crystal, grows until it joins with others or becomes so big on its own that it falls out of the sky.

It's easy to see, then, that the ice that forms at ground level in a large amount of water forms where there are lots of water molecules pressing against one another. It forms under pressure and is therefore far more solid than snow, which is made up of snowflakes that have lots of air trapped in the structure of their crystal pattern and between each flake or clump.

That's all very well and explains what we already knew – ice is hard and snow is soft – but both are really slippery, or are they?

In fact, snow is really quite grippy stuff compared with ice. You can easily stand on a steep slope that is covered in fresh snow. You'd have a much harder time standing on the same slope covered in a fresh sheet of ice, and the reason is all to do with friction.

Friction is basically resistance, or drag. Just as we came across air resistance with Britain's Fastest Bike and the Human Powered Aircraft, and water resistance with our Hydroplaning Motorbike, what we are dealing with here is resistance between two solid objects – friction. Friction provides grip, which is what gave me traction on the bike tyres in previous challenges. Far less traction, remember, on water than on solid ground. What friction also does is to generate heat. Try rubbing your hands together. Press them hard together and you can feel the resistance. You can also feel the heat. The kinetic energy (movement) is being transformed into, among other things, heat and sound energy. It's the heat that we are most interested in, because that has a direct bearing on why snow and ice are slippery.

There have been a number of theories over the years about exactly why ice is slippery. Some scientists have suggested that the surface of a sheet of ice is not under the same sort of pressure as the frozen water within the ice, so it does not bond in the same way, allowing 'loose' particles on the surface. A more common theory is that the pressure of your foot standing on the ice, and the friction you cause when your foot tries to grip the ice as you attempt to walk, melts the very surface of the ice, creating a thin layer of water between your foot and the ice.

Try rubbing your hands together again, only this time wet them first. There is far less resistance, far less friction, far less grip. Your hands are slippery when wet, the water providing lubrication. The ice beneath your foot quickly re-freezes once you have walked away – or fallen on your backside, at which point your hands, your bottom and your heels will all be trying to grip the ice, melting their own little patches, and, well, you're now in a proper state, aren't you?

The only good thing about falling over on ice is that, if you take it nice and easy, you can generally get back up again, or at least crawl away until you can find somewhere to stand up that isn't covered in ice. Snow is a very different kettle of fish. If you fall over in deep snow – not just up-to-your-knees deep, but the kind of right-over-your-head deep snow that you find on a mountainside – you sink straight in. A

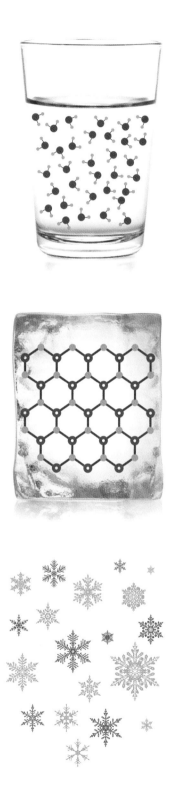

skier who falls over in loose snow that is a couple of metres deep can find himself in real trouble. Because loose snow has so much air in it, it compacts when the skier tries to put his hand down to push himself up, and his hand sinks in. Before he fell over he was far better off because his skis, as wide as his feet but far longer, spread his weight over a much bigger area, so the snow could support him without compacting as much.

Now we were starting to get to the bottom of the question about why the expensive toboggan didn't go as well in deep snow as a little lad sitting on a bin-liner. The toboggan's runners cut into the snow, and resistance from the surrounding snow on the structure of the toboggan and any parts of the rider that were in contact with it meant that it was stuck there. On the bin-liner, however, the rider was spreading his weight more, so he didn't sink in so far and gravity was still able to drag him down the slope.

On an icy slope, however, things would be different. The lad on the bin-bag would be off like a shot, riding on that thin film of water under his bum – but he would have no control whatsoever. Any slight bump or shifting of his weight would send him shooting off at an odd angle. The toboggan's runners would cut into the ice, providing friction along their length

Top: Water molecules have lots of energy and tumble about, constantly forming and breaking bonds with each other.

Middle: At 0° Celsius the water molecules have less energy and form permanent bonds, creating ice.

Bottom: Ice has a crystal structure and when it forms in air, the crystals can grow into snowflakes, none of which look the same.

and a little up the sides as well, enough to give the rider some control. By moving his weight to dig the left runner in further than the right, he would create more friction on the left, causing it to go more slowly than the runner on the right, and turning the toboggan in that direction.

What that all meant to me was that if I was going to be on ice I would have wanted to use runners. Even if I was going for straight-line speed, thin runners would keep me on course, whereas wider tracks – skis – could tend to drift sideways, robbing me of straight-line speed and generally proving difficult to control. However, I was going to be riding a sled on snow, and using skis as runners. The snow would not be deep and powdery; it would be hard packed on a ski run but would still have more 'give' to it than pure ice.

Compacting the snow beneath them and causing friction by moving across it, a skiers skis ride on a temporary film of water. The power generated by the friction beneath the skis of a normal skier on an average piste has been calculated at around 300 watts, more than enough to melt a bit of snow. To turn, skiers transfer their weight and tilt the skis so the edges of the skis bite into the snow, creating the extra friction that makes the ski grip. The way that the ski is shaped and the way that it flexes under the weight of the skier also help it to turn. Given that I was to be going for straight-line speed, however, I wasn't aiming to have to do much turning.

Nick Hamilton and the lads in Sheffield were more than happy to use their experience and technical know-how to help design a record-breaking supersled. Nick explained that skis used for speed skiing events, where the piste is a straight run down the mountainside, were generally longer and wider than normal skis, to give them good stability at high speed. The bases of the skis are not only waxed to repel the water created by the friction, allowing them to ride the water as fast as possible, but they also have a kind of tread pattern that forces the water out the back of the ski, again to help push harder and faster down the slope.

But it wasn't only friction on the snow that I would have to deal with – our old enemy air resistance would come into play as well. One of Nick's colleagues, John Hart, is a senior sports Computational Fluid Dynamics (CFD) engineer with the CSER team and an expert on aerodynamics. John explained that, just as it had been a major factor on the Britain's Fastest Bike challenge, drag would play a part in the supersled record as well. I didn't think it would be wise to ask Dave Jenkins if he would be willing to drive his racing truck down a ski run in front of me – the danger being that he might just have said yes! – so we had to consider other possible ways of minimising drag.

Speed skiers use skin-tight lycra costumes (sometimes with a special plastic coating), wear streamlined helmets that would make Darth Vader green with envy and even have aerodynamic fairings on their ski boots. I hadn't given any thought to what I would wear – I never really do – but our supersled was going to have to be as aerodynamic as possible. John had a few ideas about how that might work. In the meantime, if I was to ride a record-breaking supersled, I needed a few tips about hurtling downhill head first.

Drag, as we know, is a form of friction caused by an object, in this case the supersled rubbing against and pushing aside air particles. To combat this air resistance the supersled fairing needs to be a smooth, streamlined shape – even polishing it will help it to slip through the air more easily.

Drag

Friction between the snow and the base of the skis creates heat that melts a very thin layer of snow under the skis. This creates a thin layer of water that provides the lubrication needed to allow the skis to slide on the snow. Once the skis have passed over this thin water layer the snow re-freezes.

The supersled's fairing
will help me to glide
through the air more
easily but my helmet and
clothes will also create air
resistance. To minimise
this I will need to wear a
body-hugging suit, just
like a speed skier.

Gravity tries to pull me
straight down towards
the centre of the Earth,
but with the mountain
in the way I am dragged
down the slope instead.
Wide, long skis will help
to spread my weight and
stop me from sinking into
the snow as it compacts
beneath me.

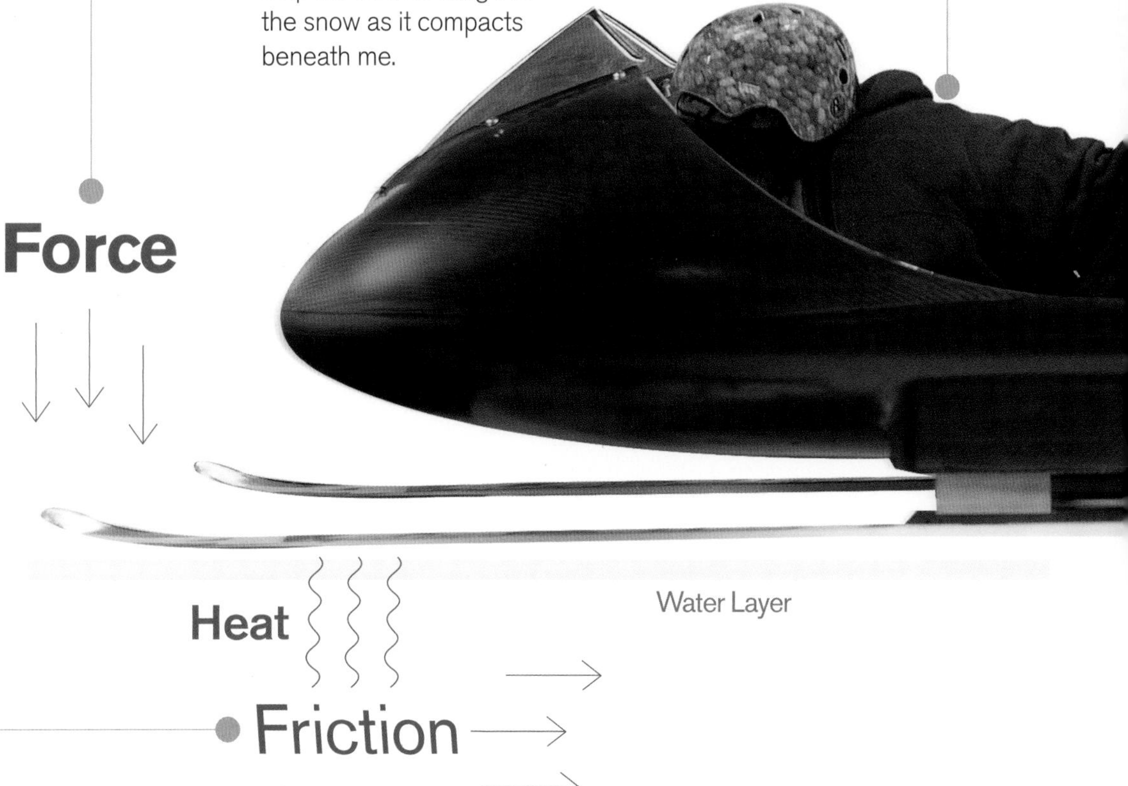

Force

Water Layer

Heat

Friction

Riding the Cresta Run

Getting up to Speed

Before the record attempt I needed to get in a bit of practice hurtling down a slope at high speed. And where better than the iconic Cresta Run.

THE Kulm Hotel has been home to the St Moritz Tobogganing Club since it was founded in 1887 by Major Bulpett, three years after he built the first Cresta Run along with volunteers from the hotel's 'Outdoors Entertainment Committee'. The club's annual medal ceremonies are still held in the hotel's Sunny Bar, and one man who is certainly no stranger to those ceremonies is Clifton Hugh Lancelot de Verdon Wrottesley, 6th Baron Wrottesley. Lord Wrottesley, who is involved in finance, spends part of the year in London and most of the rest of his time in St Moritz, where he is one of the most successful competitors ever to point his head down the Cresta Run. Racing on the Cresta Run is only for those who are members of the St Moritz Tobogganing Club (SMTC), but beginners are allowed to have a go during certain morning sessions providing that they have attended the briefing sessions and paid the appropriate fees. I had stumped up the cash and was ready to give it a go to find out just what I was letting myself in for with this downhill supersled lark.

Lord Wrottesley agreed to meet me and give me some advice on how best to tackle the Cresta Run. Standing in front of the trophy cabinet in his home, you couldn't help but be impressed. I've seen some silverware in my time and picked up a trophy or two myself, but

Top: Lord Wrottesley celebrates after setting a new 'Flying Junction' record.

Bottom: All of the Cresta Run virgins like me had to attend a safety briefing before we were allowed anywhere near the course.

his lordship's haul was a sight to behold. There are four 'classic' Cresta Run races each year and he has won each of them a record number of times. He also holds the 'Flying Junction' record for the fastest timed run starting from Top (you can guess where that is) but actually timed from Junction, which is a lower starting point on the run – 31.44 seconds. A very fast run from Junction to Finish (which you can also probably guess is the bottom), starting off at Junction without the benefit of building up

Above: The Cresta Run Clubhouse, where I was to learn about becoming a tobogganist.

speed from Top, will take around 45 seconds. A complete novice is not allowed to go from Top but can go from Junction and, if he doesn't go shooting off the run, will make it to Finish in something between 65 and 75 seconds. Now that's still going to feel very fast.

While he thought that I was 'mad as a box of snakes' for planning to break the world speed record on my supersled, Lord Wrottesley was full of encouragement about me having a go on his beloved Cresta Run. He advised me to pay close attention at the briefing, especially when it came to learning the basic moves that would help me to transfer my weight and steer the toboggan. Those who ride the Cresta Run, he explained, use toboggans and are known as riders or tobogganists. To me that sounded a bit like someone who sells fags and cigars, but it actually marks an important difference between those who ride the Cresta Run and those who take part in bobsleigh or luge races. Those who ride bobsleighs are called bobsledders and, unlike bobsleighs, the Cresta toboggans have no steering gear or brakes and are for single riders. Luge riders are often referred to as 'sliders' and, unlike the luge, you ride the Cresta Run head first, not feet first. The closest thing to a Cresta toboggan is the skeleton bob, but on bobsleigh courses where you might see the skeleton bob in action the banking on the run is curled over to help hold the toboggan on the course. The ten corners on the Cresta Run are actually designed to throw you off the course if you aren't able to steer the toboggan and control its speed.

Lord Wrottesley wished me luck, told me to enjoy the experience, warned me not to try to go too fast first time out and told me to watch out for the bend that they called Shuttlecock. The speed, of course, was what I was there for. Doing the Cresta Run was the best way to get me used to travelling down a slope, head first on my belly, with the ground rushing past just a couple of inches from my nose. That was

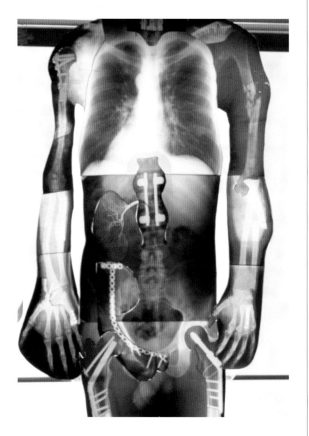

Above: The Cresta Run injury skeleton with what looks like a man with a moustache wearing a shirt and tie in his stomach.

something that I wanted to experience as part of my preparations for the supersled record.

The following day, having already applied to the SMTC to take part in a beginners' session, I trudged up through the snow to the clubhouse at 7.45 a.m. – reporting three-quarters of an hour before the run was due to open, as instructed. I was then issued with a helmet, knee pads, elbow pads, hand guards and boots with special spikes sticking out of the toes. Remember Rosa Klebb in *From Russia with Love* trying to put the boot in on Sean Connery with a poison-tipped dagger sticking out from the toe cap? She'd have loved these boots. The spikes, as I was about to learn, are your brakes and your steering gear. To guide the toboggan, also referred to as a 'bucket', round the bends, you shift your weight, going from the normal downhill position of both hands gripping at the front of the bucket to having one hand gripping at the rear down by your thigh. With your left hand back, you can lean left and guide the bucket left. Touching your left-foot spikes on the ice will also help you to turn left.

Before I, or any of the other beginners, were allowed on to the course, we had to attend the briefing in the clubhouse, where it was explained to us exactly why what we were about to do was so dangerous. Over the years the Cresta Run has broken every bone in the human body (not all on the same bloke, but they did have a skeleton image made up of different X-rays to prove that all of the bones had been done) and pulped quite a few major organs into the bargain. There have been four deaths on the run, which I thought was quite a good safety

Top: Helmet on. Right, let's get cracking!

Bottom: Ready for the off and . . . you want me to wear what?

Above: I seemed to start off slowly, but the speed certainly picked up.

record considering that people have been riding it for nearly 130 years. I say people, but what I actually mean is men. Women were banned from riding the Cresta Run when the club members took a vote on it in 1929, deciding that it was too dangerous for the fair sex, and the members have never lifted the ban. Over the years, more than half a million descents of the run have been made and there have been 28,000 crashes. You'll know what I was thinking – 'Twenty-eight thousand and one, coming up!' We were told that we should 'rake', meaning dig our spikes in, for the first part of our run, otherwise we would reach Shuttlecock going far too fast and that would be where our run would end!

Filing out to the run, we had to collect a bucket and wait for our names to be called. The

bucket is a fairly heavy piece of kit, weighing around 50 kilograms (about 110 pounds). It has a padded seat on top which slides back and forwards a bit to help you transfer your weight, but apart from that it's a simple steel frame supporting two runners – nothing fancy, but it is the thing that everyone learning how to ride the Cresta Run starts out on. As we all stood at the side of the run there was another briefing when we were shown how to rake and steer, with the instructor or 'guru' going through the first run in detail and warning us all that we would have to rake almost all the way. If we didn't rake, we would crash. We were all left in no doubt that if we didn't do as we were told we wouldn't be allowed to finish all three of the runs we were scheduled to do. I guess that's why they have such a good safety record. If you don't stick to the rules, you're out. When my name was called, I hauled my bucket up to the start point, stepped down into the run and heaved the toboggan in after me. I don't think that I was feeling nervous, just anxious to get on with it at last. I lay face down on the seat and the starting bell clanged. I lifted my spikes out of the ice and I was off. I'd hardly gone a couple of metres when I could hear them calling 'Rake!' I dragged the spikes along the ice, but the bucket carried on picking up speed along the Junction Straight. I was raking more seriously by the time that I swept into Rise, which is the first corner, and I was now starting to get a proper feeling of speed. On the straights the run is just over a metre wide (about four feet) and you can see the low ice walls rushing past you out of the corners of your eyes. Then, when you hit a curve, you swoop round a higher wall of ice before dropping back into the half-pipe run again.

On the straights the run is just over a metre wide (about four feet) and you can see the low ice walls rushing past you out of the corners of your eyes.

The Cresta Run is unique in that it is a natural ice run – the only run of its kind in the world. It is seasonal, rebuilt each year using the earth banks on the hillside and fresh snow, which is then compacted and sprayed with water to turn it to ice. The run starts in St Moritz and winds through the ten turns down a valley to what used to be the village of Cresta, now part of the district of Celerina. The steepness of the slope ranges from 1 in 8.7 to 1 in 2.8.

I felt like I was going fast, but I knew that I probably wasn't. What I really wanted to be able to do was to steer the bucket properly, and that, clearly, is something that you can do best when you really are going fast. By the time I

was approaching the bottom half of the run I had eased off the raking. You can take the bottom of the course a lot faster, but steering the bucket was still frustrating me. Either it wouldn't steer at all, or it was hyper-sensitive. There are proper skills to be learned here. I was happy to have made it all the way down, but I suddenly found that I was breathing really hard, like I had just stepped off Britain's Fastest Bike!

Why was I so out of puff when I came off the run? It's not as though I had actually sprinted all the way down, after all. I had been lying on the bucket. Some of that breathlessness will have been due to the altitude. There is less oxygen in the air up in the mountains, so you puff harder when you're doing any kind of exercise. Most of it, though, was due to the fact that I had been tensed up all the way down. I had been holding every muscle tight as I tried to pull the bob this way and that. Still doesn't sound like I should have been out of breath? Then give this a go.

Providing that you are fit and able and aren't suffering from a bad back or anything like that (don't come crying to me if you do yourself a mischief), lie face down on the floor. Now tuck your elbows in with your hands facing forwards and raise your upper body. Next, keeping your body perfectly straight, raise yourself up on your toes as well so that your chest, stomach, knees and legs are parallel to the ground. Don't stick your bum in the air. Then see how long you can hold yourself there. It's an exercise called 'the bridge' and it's used to help improve your core strength, the muscles in your torso and your legs. You have to keep everything tense, and after a while it is knackering.

Another one to try – very simple: just stand on one leg and raise the other one up and down.

It's not the leg that you're lifting and lowering that gets tired, it's the one that is holding all of your weight. Muscles like to contract and then release, like springs. If you tense up a muscle and hold it there, then you need to supply it with energy for it to carry on doing its job. We know from the previous chapters that your blood carries oxygen to your muscles to fuel them, and tensed-up muscles are asking for lots of oxygen. That's why you can get out of breath doing 'the bridge' or standing on one leg, and that's why I was panting like a St Bernard when I came off the Cresta Run.

Lord Wrottesley would surely not have had the same problem. He would stay far more relaxed on the run. You need to be relaxed if you are to use your muscles properly, not tight as a drum. Staying relaxed was something that I would have to concentrate on when I took to the snow on my supersled. 'Staying chilled' was how I was going to put it, but that sounds a bit daft when you're up a mountain in the Alps, standing on a snow field, doesn't it? Also, I would have to remember to breathe. I barely took a breath coming down the Cresta Run, and that's not the best way to keep your muscles relaxed.

On my second run I was struggling to make the bucket go where I wanted it to. I held back on the raking on the upper part of the course and before I knew it I was hurtling towards the infamous Shuttlecock. I knew it was coming. I could see it. I leaned and I raked but the bucket shot straight up the banking and out over the top, with me clinging on. 'Get rid of the thing,' had been Lord Wrottesley's advice if I was going to crash. 'Push it out in front of

Left: Crashing out into the straw at Shuttlecock.

you, because you don't want it smashing into you from behind.' It seemed fair advice to me – I've baled off a few motorbikes in my time for exactly the same reason – but the next thing I knew I was ploughing through soft snow and scattered straw, the straw having been put there precisely to catch speedsters like me when they crashed out at Shuttlecock. I came to a fairly gentle stop and, thankfully, didn't need any X-rays that could be added to the clubhouse skeleton! I was seeing an improvement, though, so for the final run I really went for it. It was a case of 'More speed, Captain!' and I was a bit happier with the result. I was achieving respectably average times for a beginner.

> I could now claim to be a member of the Shuttlecock Club, which is exclusively for riders who have crashed at Shuttlecock.

I could now claim to be a member of the Shuttlecock Club, which is exclusively for riders who have crashed at Shuttlecock. Among my fellow members is RAF Wing Commander Andy Green, the first man to break the sound barrier on land – he did that in the jet-powered Thrust car, not at Shuttlecock – and, of course, Lord Wrottesley, who was once Shuttlecock Club President. As a Shuttlecock Club member I was entitled to buy the club tie at the SMTC clubhouse, and I duly did, even though it's a rare day when I'm seen wearing a tie! It was a fine souvenir of my time in St Moritz on the Cresta Run.

Above: I qualified for a Shuttlecock Club tie after crashing on the infamous bend.

Top left: Left hand back and right hand forward to shift my weight coming into a bend.

Top right: When you are just centimetres away from the ice wall, you get a very good impression of the speed you are doing.

Bottom left: Trees cast shadows over the track which can make it difficult to judge the bends.

Bottom right: Going for it flat out, feet up, no raking . . .

Following page: Weight on the left, leaning into a bend at speed.

Building a Record Breaker

Now that I had a good idea about what it is like to shoot head first down a mountain and had learned a little about the do's and don'ts of tobogganing, what I really needed was a supersled that would be fast enough to take the world record.

I NEEDED to see what Nick Hamilton and his team at Sheffield Hallam University had come up with. At a workshop at the University, Nick explained that what we needed to create was something that was heavy enough to be stable (the Cresta buckets weighed around 50 kilos, remember) when it was travelling downhill at speed. Ski slopes look beautifully smooth from a distance, but up close they are scattered with lumps of icy snow created by the tracks of the machines that are used to groom the pistes, as well as small bumps that reflect the fact that the snow is lying over a slope that is part of the mountain terrain. No ski slope is ever as smooth as the icing on a cake, and that's why skiers ski with their knees bent. They can transfer their weight more easily when they flex their knees, and bending their knees also allows them to use their legs as shock absorbers to deal with the bumps. Absorbing minor impacts by bending

Top: The raking teeth used as brakes were ultimately sited further back on the chassis, to take advantage of my weight bearing down on them, and operated using a bicycle chain linkage.

Bottom: This kind of flag is normally attached to aircraft air speed indicators or the tips of missiles — I wouldn't be going quite that fast!

their knees, they can avoid being thrown off course and off balance. Building any kind of suspension system into the sled would make it more complex and probably end up adding too much weight, so my only shock absorber would be the foam padding on the sled's seat, but making the whole sled robust enough would help to hold me on course.

With that in mind, we decided to use box-section steel tubing to create a simple, square chassis. At the sides, the steel cross members would stick out a bit to allow us to mount the two skis that were to act as our runners as far apart as we wanted. This was important to give us the ideal weight distribution. If you watch someone skiing for fun on an average slope, they will have their skis quite close together, especially if they are on a slope where they are negotiating humps, called moguls, in the snow. They want to keep their skis together so that they can easily transfer their weight from one ski to the other in order to turn. If you watch a downhill racer, you will see them stand taller, with their skis closer together, when they are turning, but when they are cruising down a straight section they adopt the 'tuck' position, hunkering down with their chest on their thighs, and their skis further apart for even weight distribution and to keep the skis flat on the snow. Flat means less drag, more speed. Speed skiers, who go straight downhill, use the tuck position all the time. We needed to find the ideal width to set our skis for the best weight distribution and stability, hence the longer cross members, which would allow us to move the mounting

Top: Looking through the very familiar motorcycle fairing on the supersled during construction.

Bottom: Taking a few rough edges off the carbon fibre bodywork of the main fairing.

brackets further in or out as required. Trial and error would ultimately decide exactly where they went, but having the inside edges of the skis at about shoulder width seemed a good place to start.

Flat means less drag, more speed. Speed skiers, who go straight downhill, use the tuck position all the time.

Normally, skis are attached to the skier, using bindings that clip on to and grip the flanges at the front and back of the boot. The bindings are also spring-loaded and can fly open if the skier falls. That way the skis detach and are not digging in to the snow, twisting joints and breaking bones as the unlucky skier goes tumbling down the mountain. I didn't need anything like that, so we were able to fabricate simple steel brackets that we could screw on to the skis and bolt on to the chassis.

Once we had all of our components planned and prepared, we measured the steel, cut the lengths and I was able to do a bit of welding to create the chassis. On top of the chassis, all we needed was a simple wooden board, a bit of spongy foam to create a cushion and some vinyl cloth to cover it all up and stop the foam soaking up too much water from melted snow. I thought that was it, job done, but the Sheffield lads has another idea that they wanted to try out.

They showed me how we could create a brake by mounting two lever handles at the front of the sled which, when I pulled back on them, would turn an axle running across the sled below the seat. Attached to the axle would be a series of ten steel fingers with cog-like teeth cut into the ends. The teeth would dig into the snow, and the harder I pulled, the harder they would dig in. My sled was to have built-in rakes, so I wouldn't have to wear anything like the Rosa Klebb boots that I had to use on the Cresta Run. The rake-brake was such a simple design that, once we had cut the teeth into the end of one steel finger, we could use it as a template and the whole thing was ready to be fitted in no time.

I have to say that, apart from the skis, which were proper racing jobs and were beautifully finished, my racing sled didn't look very pretty. I didn't mind that at all. I was after speed – this wasn't a beauty competition. Meanwhile John Hart had other concerns. What we had built was certain to go downhill quite fast, but it was far from being aerodynamic. The way things were, I would be lying face down on the sled but my upper body, the front of the seat and the flat sections of the chassis as well as the ski brackets would be acting a bit like the screen we built on to the back of Dave Jenkins's racing truck. Remember this?

Left: Examining one of the kilns where the carbon fibre components are cured – a big enough oven to take anyone's Christmas turkey!

A Steer from Amy Williams

You can never get too much advice when you're trying out something new, providing that your advice comes from people who know what they're talking about, and Olympic Gold Medallist Amy Williams certainly knows her stuff.

AMY is an athlete who started out as a runner, competing in the 400 metres event. She was good, too, but was slightly off the pace when it came to making it into the national team. Then she was introduced to the skeleton bob, and she never looked back. Don't say it, I know, you *have* to keep looking forward on those things. At the 2010 Winter Olympics in Vancouver Amy won her gold medal – the only medal that came home to Britain from Canada.

Amy had a look over the sled. It wasn't a patch on the Blackroc skeleton that she had raced in Vancouver. That had been designed by a team at Southampton University led by engineers Rachel Blackburn and James Roche, which is where the Blackroc Project got its name, although the actual sled was called Arthur. The Blackroc team, with the help of our guys from Sheffield Hallam, had spent four years designing, building, testing and refining Arthur. We didn't have anything like that sort of time to play with and, in any case, we were going to be running on snow, not on the ice of a bobsleigh track. Amy could see where we were coming from and gave the vinyl seat a prod. When she lay on Arthur, he was specially formed to mould to the contours of her body. If anything, our supersled prototype looked a bit too comfy!

Above: Olympic Skeleton Bob Gold Medal winner Amy Williams gave me a few tips about hurtling down a slope head first.

Amy had me lie on a bench and got me balancing on my torso so that I could feel how best to shift my weight. She steered Arthur by pressing down with one shoulder and the opposite knee to get the right sort of shift in weight. I was hoping that I wouldn't have to steer at all, but if course corrections were needed I was picking up plenty of tips on technique. We chatted for a while about her sport and how she had been terrified when she first tried the skeleton, but that and the thrill of the speed were what got her hooked. In Vancouver she was hitting 90 mph on Arthur during her gold medal run and wore

an aerodynamic bodysuit to give her the best streamlined shape. She also had special ridges on her helmet to make it more aerodynamic, and there were complaints about that from the opposition. The complaints were rejected by the Olympic authorities, who had already approved Amy's helmet, but it does show how seriously you need to take aerodynamics when split-second times are involved.

To try out Amy's tips, of course, we needed a slope with a bit of snow on it. Summer weather in Britain is usually something that people have a good moan about, but even the most pessimistic weatherman wasn't forecasting snow in Sheffield in June 2013. To test out our prototype, we needed to head north – not to the Arctic, just to Castleford.

Above: With the skis off, a few minor adjustments are made to the brakes during testing.

Below: With a warm brew in the boot room for a bit of a chat with Amy.

Above: Amy was more than happy to talk me through what high-speed sledding is all about. I, of course, was more than happy to listen.

Castleford is home to one of the UK's three Xscape centres. The emphasis at Xscape is on fun and at Castleford they have a cinema, a bowling alley, a battleground where you can hunt your mates down and shoot each other with lasers, climbing walls and all sorts of other things, including the Snozone, an indoor slope where you can learn to ski on real snow.

The Snozone slopes are created in a huge, hangar-like hall where they keep the overall temperature down to between -2º and -3º Celsius, although when they are making snow they can drop the temperature as low as -6º. Making snow? Yes, they make their own snow – up to 1,700 tonnes of the white stuff covering the 170-metre long slope. The slope is a concrete slab covered with a layer of insulation on top of which run lines of 20 mm pipes. The pipes have a very cold anti-freeze solution flowing through them and when water is run over the pipes it freezes to make a layer of ice – a bit like an ice rink on a slope. Water and air are then sprayed at high pressure through snow cannons, creating a fine mist of moisture, which freezes in the air and falls onto the slope as snow. The same sort of snow cannons are used in ski resorts to create snow when there hasn't been enough natural snowfall.

Snozone were happy for us to show up after they had officially closed one evening so that our film crew wouldn't be disturbing anyone and we would have the slope to ourselves to try out the sled.

Right: It might look like I was getting far too comfy, but I was just following instructions and benefiting from a bit of coaching!

Indoor Snow
Testing and Modifying

I learned a lot listening to Amy in the Snozone boot room, but I couldn't wait to get out on the slope and give the prototype a run.

THE team from Sheffield was there, of course. They were as keen as me to get out on the snow, and we carried the sled to the slope together. If I'm honest, at this point we were probably all feeling a bit like kids in the park on a snowy afternoon!

We started off only part of the way up the slope, to make sure that I wasn't going to go thundering into the wall at the end of the flat run-out area at the bottom of the slope. The wall was all padded and no one expected that I would overshoot the run-out, but we took things one step at a time anyway. The sled actually rode incredibly well. I could turn a bit by leaning and the brakes did a very good job. Now I could feel the excitement that little kids have when they're out on their plastic sleds. They run back up the slope, they're so desperate to have another go. Fortunately, I didn't have to do that as Snozone has a moving carpet conveyor belt on the ground at the side of the slope as well as a drag lift to get you back up there without knackering you.

I went again and again, from higher up, trying different positions and little changes of technique. Going up and down the slope, I didn't pay much heed to the temperature. I was keeping fine and warm. The film crew, on the other hand, were doing a lot of standing around and, with the temperature in the Snozone hovering around -6º, they were feeling the cold. I suppose I can count that as payback for all the

Top: The boot room coaching continued when we were out on the Xscape snow.

Bottom: I'm not sure that helmet was impressing Amy much.

Top: Heaving the prototype up the slope with the help of the lads from Sheffield and the lass from Bath.

Bottom: The prototype had two grab handles for me to hold on to, with the brake lever behind my right hand.

times they've made me do daft things like borrowing someone's bathroom scales!

We had a timing system set up on the slope that gave a readout of my speed, and as I got more confident the speed began to creep higher. Apart from having my chin inches from the ground, the prototype felt nothing like the bucket on the Cresta Run. It was solid and controllable, with none of the bucket's twitchiness. The sled held its line going down the slope and I didn't have the feeling that it wanted to slither off sideways.

I managed speeds of around 30 mph, but never actually felt that I was going very fast, which tended to make me think that the sled was going to be capable of far higher speeds. Considering the length of the Snozone slope and the fact that I would be on a far longer and steeper run when I was going for the record, riding a sled that had far better slipstreaming, I thought that the test session was really encouraging. Onwards and upwards!

Left: The briefings here weren't quite as serious as in St Moritz!

Following page: Touching the brakes at the end of a run.

Top: Feet up for speed on the first run.

Middle: Leaning right and cutting into the snow.

Bottom: We had a timer set up on the slope to find out just how fast the prototype would go.

The Supersled Takes Shape

With the help of the carbon fibre experts at epm:technology the supersled was starting to come together.

IN CHARGE of the supersled project at epm:technology was Andy Butt, an engineer with years of experience in working with carbon fibre and just the man to explain why it was the stuff we should be using for our fairing. The answer is that it's a miracle material that engineers and designers absolutely love. If we were to make our fairing for the supersled out of steel – and most car body panels are still made from steel – it wouldn't be as strong, it wouldn't be as stiff and it wouldn't be as light. Carbon fibre is five times stronger than steel, twice as stiff and only one third of the weight. Saving weight might not have been such an issue when we were putting together the prototype chassis, but if we now added too much weight it might work to slow the sled.

Carbon fibre's secret is in the way that it is made. A carbon fibre product starts off as very thin strands of carbon – thinner than a human hair. These are twisted together to form a kind of yarn, a bit like cotton fibres are spun to make thread. The big difference is that the carbon yarn is far tougher stuff and, when it is woven into a cloth, it is well on the way to becoming strong enough to be used in the bodywork of a Formula One car or a jet airliner.

Turning a textile substance that is delivered to factories and workshops on long rolls into something stronger than steel is actually quite simple. A mould is created rather like a jelly mould, although the mould they use at

Above: The carbon fibre has a smooth, shiny, tough finish when it comes out of the mould.

epm:technology to create the parts for the supersled is more like a kind of plaster that can be shaped, drilled or carved very accurately to achieve the right shape. The mould is coated with a very thin film of release agent that will allow the finished carbon-fibre part to be separated from the mould cleanly and easily, and then the carbon-fibre cloth is laid over the mould. The cloth is tucked in to all of the mould's nooks and crannies, and multiple layers of cloth are used to build up the thickness and strength of the finished part.

In industry, most carbon-fibre cloth is impregnated with the correct amount of epoxy resin – which acts like varnish or glue and will soak into the carbon fibres, binding them together and then 'curing', or hardening. The alternative is to paint the epoxy resin on to each layer of the carbon-fibre cloth before curing it.

Above: Preparing the basic chassis, with brakes attached, to receive its streamlined bodywork.

Right: Sanding the carbon fibre creates black dust that makes wearing a mask a must.

Top: Drilling holes to allow the Perspex fairing to be mounted on the nose cone.

Bottom: With the foam 'bed' in place and the skis on, the supersled was pretty much complete.

For our carbon-fibre parts, the epoxy resin was cured first by sealing the component and its mould in a plastic bag and then pumping out the air. When the carbon fibre and mould are vacuum sealed together in this way, the pressure of the outside air forces the cloth to follow the exact shape of the mould. The whole lot is then heat treated – baked in a kiln so that the epoxy resin is activated and cures, setting the carbon fibre into the shape we wanted.

The result is a smooth, shiny surface where the carbon fibre has been formed against the mould, although you can still see and feel the fibre patterns on the inside of your new component. For anything like a car body panel, aircraft bodywork or our supersled, the smooth outer surface is what matters most, because it plays such a huge part in minimising drag. Andy had actually suggested a modification to the design that John Hart had come up with, making the fairing more like a motorbike fairing, so that I could look up – with my eyes, that is, not sticking my head out into the slipstream to look – and see where I was going, and that wasn't the only design modification that was being taken into consideration.

The supersled was to have a number of new additions. Its fairing would streamline me, the forward area of the sled and the ski brackets. In fact, Andy had suggested that the whole sled could be made from carbon fibre, and this option was being taken under consideration. As well as the brakes that would rake the snow under the front end of the sled, the Sheffield team had also come up with the idea of fitting another braking device – a parachute. It would be attached to a boom that would reach out beyond my legs, so that I didn't get tangled up in the parachute lines, and I would be able to deploy it as an emergency brake.

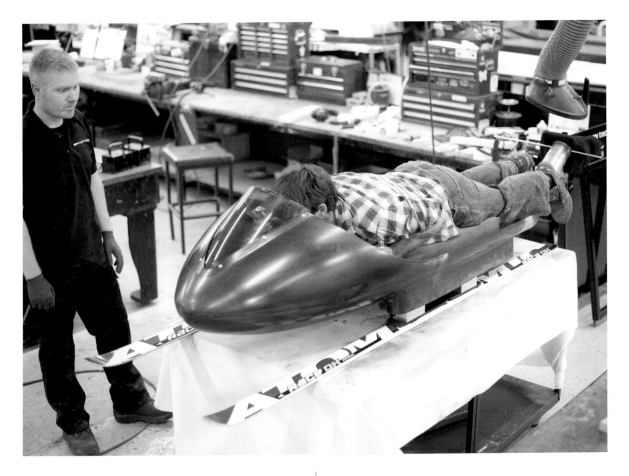

Above: Trying out the supersled for size on a workshop bench.

We had time to consider all of these things, because the one thing that we didn't have at our disposal was a snow slope where we could go for the record. In Britain the mountain slopes where we might have found a suitable ski run don't really open for business until December, if they have had sufficient snowfall. In Europe there are several ski resorts where summer skiing on glaciers is not only possible but hugely popular, and there are slopes with snow on them throughout the year. The glacier ski runs, however, are not always ideal for speed skiing. Any of the European speed ski runs that are used for competitions would have been ideal for our record attempt – these are steep, fast slopes. All we needed now was snow.

So I was left watching the weather and snow reports, like a kid staring out through the curtains – waiting impatiently for the first flakes of snow to fall. When they did, I'd be packing an extra pair of socks and my supersled and heading for the mountains!

Index

Page numbers in *italic* refer
to the illustrations

carbon fibre 105, 244–6, *244–5*

cars: drag racers 101–2

    hydroplaning 142, 146–7

    motor pacing 21, 38

    slipstreaming 28–9

Castera, Jean-Eugene-André *17*

Castleford 235–6, 238–41

cavitation effect 158, 160–1, *160–1*

Centre for Sports Engineering Research
(CSER) 212, 215

centrifugal force 175

Charles River race track, Boston 18

Chase Terrace Technology College,
Staffordshire 168–71, *168–70*

Chasewater Reservoir 172–5, *172*

Chevrolet 22

City Airport, London 172

cockpits, human-powered aircraft 104

Commonwealth Games, Alberta (1978)
58

Coniston Water 144, *144*

Continental tyres 48

Cotic mountain bikes 13

Cresta Run *205*, *207*, 209–10, 211, 211,
218–26, *218–29*

Crete 80

Crystal Palace, London 17

D

Daedalus 77, 80

Daedalus, HMS 88

Dambusters 142, 143

Davis, Graham 150, 156–8, 175, 176, 178,
184, 189

Daytona 500 race 28–9

De Havilland Aircraft Company 84, *86*

De Havilland Mosquito 84, *85*

Derby 32

Didier, Paul *83*

dirt bikes 139–40

disc brakes, bicycles 51, *51*

Dodds, F.L. 16

dolphins: aquaplaning 165

bow-riding 35

    slipstreaming *34–5*

drag (air resistance): aquaplaning *167*

    bicycles 14

    birds *119*

    flying 94, *96*, *98*

    friction 213–14

    horse racing 33

    hydroplaning 143, 147, *149*

    slipstreaming 25–6, 27, 28

    supersled 215

drag racers 101–2

Dragon F1 boat 172–5, *173*

Dragon Powerboats 172

Drumlanrig Castle 16

Dunlop 17

Dynamiq Engineering 34

E

Eilmer of Malmesbury 80–1

elevators, aircraft 106, 121

Elizabeth II, Queen 32, 33

Elkes, Harry 18

Ellesmere Canal 188

endurance races, motor pacing 19

energy, muscles 54–5, 100–2, *103*

engines, aircraft 94

English Channel 85–6, *87*

epm:technology group 244

epoxy resin 244–6

Epsom Derby 32

ergonometers 54

eye muscles 102, *103*

F

fairings 23, 44–5, 60, 244–6, *246*

Farrah, Mo 54

feathers, bird's wings *118–19*

fish, slipstreaming 32, *33*

flight: birds 116–17, *116–19*

    gliders 88–91, *89–93*

    human-powered 74–131

    science of 94–9, *96–9*

foam, human-powered aircraft

106–11, *107*

foils: cavitation effect 160–1

    hydroplaning 142, 143

force: hydroplaning 146

    laws of motion 95, *97–8*

    slipstreaming 26

Ford Model A 20

Forlanini, Enrico 143–4, *143*

Formula One powerboat racing 168–71,
169–70, 172–5, *173*

Forrester, Dr Alex 94, 100–1, 105, 113,
121, 124

freezing 212–13

friction *97*, 213, 215

G

g-forces 175

Gadd, Trevor 58

gears: bicycles *50*, 51, 61

    human-powered flight *104*, 105, *128*

Gerhardt, Dr Frederick 83

Gerhardt Cycleplane 83, *83*

Gibson, Guy *143*

glaciers, skiing on 247

gliders 88–91, *89–93*

gliding 80–1, 82

glucose 54–5

glycogen 54

Gossamer Albatross 85–6, *87*

Gossamer Condor 2 85

gravity 95, *97*, *98*, 147

Green, Wing Commander Andy 226

ground effect, flying 116–17

Guinness World Records 142–3, 150, 156,
189, 192, 206

gyroscopic stability 147

H

Hamilton, Nick 212, 215, 230

hang-gliders 80–1, *81*

Hart, John 215, 233, 244, 246

Hatfield Puffin 84, *86*

heat, and ice 213

helmets, speed skiing 215

Acknowledgements

GUY MARTIN and North One Television would like to thank everyone who generously gave their time to help make the show and the book.

From the Britain's Fastest Bike episode, Jason Hill at Dynamiq Engineering; Dave Jenkins of Jenkins Motorsport; Brian and Jason Rourke from Rourke Cycles; cycling legend Dave Le Grys; Sarah Moseley and Rhona Pearce at Loughborough University; Graham Bristow from the British Pacing Association; Neil Barker at Sonic Communications; Mike Broadbent from Racelogic; Simon Perry and the team at Hope Technology and Olympic gold medallist Laura Trott.

From the Human Powered Aircraft episode, Chris Bill, Jacob Chong, Alex Forrester and Reuben Symons from Southampton University; Ben Tindale from Tindale Systems; glider pilot Guy Westgate; Bill Brooks, Chairman of the Royal Aeronautical Society and Alan Lassiere and Derek Piggott of the SUMPAC team.

From the Hydroplaning Motorbike episode, Charlie Broughton and Graham Davis from Sealander Marine International; Dave Main; Richard Mumford from RM Services; James Baker; Owain and Aled Charles; Mike Hopkins from Storm Geomatics; Hugh Hunt from Trinity College, Cambridge; Jonathan Jones of Dragon Powerboats; Western Waterjet and the Osprey Rescue Team.

And from the World's Fastest Sled episode, Andy Butt and James Carter from epm:technology; Nick Hamilton and John Hart from Sheffield Hallam University's Centre for Sports Engineering Research; Steve Haake; Terry Senior; Olympic gold medallist Amy Williams; Lord Clifton Wrottesley and the St. Moritz Tobogganing Club and Snozone in Castleford.

From North One Television, Alex Armstead, Nat Bullen, Brian Charles, Andrew Chorlton, Neil Duncanson, Steve Gowans, James Hey, Ewan Keil, Martyn Kilvert, Danielle McGirr, Vince Narduzzo, Tom Norton, Andrew Parkes, Amy Roff, Dionne South, Sarah Swift, Annelise Unitt, Robin Ward and James Woodroffe. From Channel 4, Jay Hunt, Ralph Lee, Yad Luthra, Nathalie Mohoboob and Sara Ramsden. And Andy Spellman.

From Virgin Books, Lorna Russell and Elen Jones; Rod Green, Barry Hayden, Charlie Magee, Dominic Cooper and Two Associates, Claire Gouldstone, Steve Dobell and James Ryan.